THE
HIGH POINT
HISTORY SERIES

AMERICAN HISTORY 1754-1945

JACE BOWER

★ ★ ★

Connect with me at

www.highpointhistoryseries.com

Like my facebook page The High Point History Series

Dedicated to my mother, without whose help,

this book would not be possible.

~J.B.

ACKNOWLEDGMENTS

I would like to express my gratitude to quite a few people. Mrs. Sivacek for coaching me through the process of writing a book; Aunt Joyce for editing; Sam, Samuel, Zach, Meghan and David for taking the time to read the book and review it; my family and grandparents for encouraging me; Dad for some general editing, giving pointers, etc; Mom for helping set up the website and preparing the book for publication; and of course, God, for giving me a love of "His-story" and the grace to write this book.

Table of Contents

List of Illustrations

Introduction

C.S. Lewis described history as "a story written by God's finger." Every once and awhile, we read history and we think "that couldn't happen by chance". The only way we can explain some historical events is through acknowledging that it was the Providence of God that led things to play out in certain ways. How else could Washington survive at the Battle of Monongahela, despite being shot over a dozen times? How else could America come into existence unless the Hand of God was lovingly, providentially, guiding it towards independence? God is always in control of all events. He works in mysterious ways.

Many of the early American founding fathers were dedicated Christ-followers. They established this nation on the principle that all men were endowed by their Creator with certain inalienable rights. They fervently believed that those nations that obeyed God received blessing and those that didn't received judgement.

This book will not report every detail of American history. It will hit what I like to call the "high points". America progressed quite far between 1754 and 1945. At the beginning of this book, you are introduced to a fledgling group of colonies ruled by a distant king across the sea. By the end, you are left with a dynamic image of a world power. It's not coincidental, it's providential. America wasn't lucky, it was blessed.

PART ONE:
1754-1860

CHAPTER ONE

THE FRENCH AND INDIAN WAR

In order to understand the American Revolution, and thus the rest of American history, we must start in 1754 with the French and Indian War.

The French and Indian War was fought between France and England. France was aided by many Native American nations while the English were aided by the American colonists. The war lasted from 1754 to 1761 and is sometimes considered an extension of the Seven Years War in Europe, despite the fact that that particular conflict did not start for another two years.

The French and Indian War was the foundation on which the nation of America was built. This conflict changed the dynamic of North America dramatically. It changed the relationship between England and the American colonies, and it led to the end of a long Anglo-French struggle for the North American continent, leaving England almost solely dominant in the American sphere until the Revolutionary

War. No war is without cause, however, and the French and Indian War is no exception.

The number one cause of this conflict between France and England was control of the Ohio territory. The French and English both claimed the region and both sent expeditions to secure the territory. When the French began building forts in Ohio, the English felt threatened. War was kindled.

Thinking More About It — What was so important about the Ohio Territory? Think about it and discuss your ideas. Research the question if you wish.

The Battle of Monongahela

One of the first battles of the French and Indian War was fought between the English along with their American colonist allies and the French and their Canadian and Native American allies. The battle was fought in what is now part of Pennsylvania. The English General Edward Braddock had arrived from England with English troops and a couple of Irish divisions in May of 1755. In June of the same year, Braddock led his army into the Ohio wilderness hoping to capture the French Fort Duqeusne. A number of Virginia militiamen under the leadership of George Washington accompanied him. Braddock, who had served in battles in the Netherlands, was not used to fighting in the wooded

American wilderness. He refused to recruit Native American scouts and he split his force up to better maneuver his artillery. This proved to be a foolish decision. The French and their Canadian militiamen and Native American allies departed from Fort Duquesne and ambushed the English in the woods around the Monongahela River. Confusion was the name of the game. The English, unused to wilderness warfare, scattered and Braddock was mortally wounded, dying soon after the battle.

THE DEATH OF GENERAL BRADDOCK AT MONONGAHELA

George Washington attempted to rally the English and colonists during the fight but his attempts proved to be in vain. However, the miraculous providence of God kept Washington safe. He was shot in the coat multiple times and yet he remained unhurt. His hat was shot off his head and two horses were also shot from under him. Only by the providence of God could this man survive, later being a phenomenal character in the creation of the United States.

Past, Present, Future — How do you see God's providence working in your life? Discuss. What are other examples from history of God's providence?

The Course of the War

France and England continued to fight for control of Ohio and the Mississippi River and the war escalated. The French were led by a veteran of the War of the Austrian Succession named Louis-Joseph de Montcalm. He was much more experienced than the English commanders and, as a result, the French won several great victories in the years following the Battle of Monongahela. These included the Battle of Fort Bull, Oswego and the fall of Fort William Henry. In 1759, the English under General James Wolfe attacked Quebec in French Canada. There they faced Montcalm's French forces on the Plains of Abraham. Both generals were killed in the conflict and the battle ended in an decisive English victory. The tide turned there at Quebec and within a few years the English had successfully defeated the French and had ousted them from North America.

THE BATTLE OF THE PLAINS OF ABRAHAM

Cool Fact

Although the French and Indian War is remembered as a struggle for the North American continent between France and England, it was part of a larger conflict. In Europe, Prussian forces joined the English and fought against France, Austria, Spain and Russia. In India, the French were ousted from their colonies by the English, and the English also attacked French and Spanish forces in the Caribbean Sea and in West Africa. It's ironic that this worldwide conflict was fought centuries before the First World War, but even this wasn't the first. Three other worldwide wars were fought between 1689-1697 (King William's War), 1701-1714 (Queen Anne's War) and 1740-1746 (King George's War).

The Results of the War

There were several major results of the French and Indian War, which later led to the American Revolution.

First, the English seized the French colonies in Canada and on the Mississippi River, effectively ousting the French from North America. This not only heightened English power in North America but also made the French bitter about their loss. They would be more than glad to come to the aid of the Colonies during the Revolution.

Second, the war, being quite costly for the English, enabled King George III to impose a tax upon the Colonies, leading the Colonists to resent English rule.

Finally, and probably most important, the war became a fire in which the Colonies' unity was forged. Having fought battles on their own and winning without English aid, the Colonists realized that they could rule themselves. And they wanted to.

Visit www.highpointhistoryseries.com/bonuses/ for FREE bonus videos.

CHAPTER TWO

THE AMERICAN REVOLUTION

Causes of the American Revolution

The American Revolution, at the outset, was caused by harsh taxes imposed by the English government and the lack of representation the colonies had in the English Parliament. However, a deeper cause for rebellion lay under the surface. It lay in the problem of differences in philosophy.

England was a monarchy and had been for centuries. Tyranny was common at the time and it was no different in England. In fact, the tyrannical rule of James I, the first English king of the Stuart dynasty, was the reason for the Pilgrims' departure from England in the first place.

Liberty was not a new concept, in fact, it was an old one. Democracy was an ancient Greek idea. Personal responsibility and equality of man were a first-century Christian concept. In fact, the liberty of the founding fathers was indeed distinctly Christian.

The cause of rebellion was not so much what England did, but rather what Americans were thinking. The basis of the American Revolution was the colonists' concept of liberty. The Pilgrims' "Matrix of Liberty" was faith, morality, law and education. The Colonists were well-grounded in the Christian faith and, therefore, they based this new nation on the following Christian principles: freedom of religion, personal responsibility, equality of man, law and order, honor and respect for man's rights and such.

They believed the English were not recognizing these rights. The English had begun to pass Tax Acts on the Colonists to pay for the French and Indian War debts. These included taxes on sugar and tea. They also passed the Writs of Assistance Act, which allowed English officials to search Colonists' houses and businesses without search warrants, the Quebec Act, which forbade the Colonists from settling the hard-won land west of the Allegheny Mountains, and the Quartering Act, which forced the colonists to house English soldiers even if they didn't want to. The colonists declared these laws to be "intolerable" and hence came the name "Intolerable Acts."

A Massachusetts colonist named Samuel Adams, along with Dr. Joseph Warren, created a group known as the Sons of Liberty to protest these new laws. They rioted and rallied against the English government. Things came to a head in 1770 when colonial hecklers were harassing an English sentry in Boston. The guard called for aid. General Thomas Gage, the English commander of English forces in Boston, sent some men to aid the guard but warned them not to fire. One man did fire after the hecklers taunted him and dared him to do so. Crispus Attucks, a freed slave, was killed and five others were as well when the other English soldiers also fired. This was called the Boston Massacre and it only served to further anger the Colonists.

In 1773, when a tax on tea passed, the Sons of Liberty took matters into their own hands. They masqueraded as Mohawk Indians and dumped the tea off English ships in Boston harbor. This became known as the Boston Tea Party, and it enraged King George III of England and the English Parliament. George III closed the Boston harbor to teach the Colonists a lesson. In 1774, the Continental Congress, a group of influential men from around the colonies, met to discuss what to do about the relations between the colonies and England. The situation worsened as winter 1774 turned to spring 1775. As the blossoms of April bloomed, so did the Colonists' attempts at rebellion.

Thinking More About It-What do you think the most important cause for the Revolution was? Were the colonists right in rebelling against England? Think about it and discuss your ideas.

Cool Fact

John Robinson, the Puritan minister who lead the Pilgrims before they set sail for America, was influential in forming the first Pilgrim governments and thus indirectly influenced the founding of America. He never set foot on the New World, on the land which would be so influenced by his ideas and leadership.

The Battles of Lexington and Concord

The Colonists began to collect weapons and supplies in preparation for an insurrection against English rule. General Thomas Gage received word in Boston that arms and ammunitions were stored in the nearby town of Concord. Also in Concord were two of the most troublesome patriots, Samuel Adams and John Hancock, whom he wished to arrest. He sent some English troops under John Pitcairn to confiscate the supplies and arrest the two men. Paul Revere, a local silversmith patriot, and two other riders, William Dawes and Dr. Samuel Prescott, rode toward Lexington to raise the alarm. They roused the local Massachusetts militiamen and then headed on to Concord to warn Adams and Hancock.

Early in the morning on April 18, 1775, the Massachusetts militiamen confronted Pitcairn's English force at Lexington. Pitcairn ordered the patriots to disperse. They began to withdraw but a mysterious shot fired by an unknown soldier exploded through the air. The English fired and eight Americans were killed. The patriots fled, and the English continued on toward Concord.

They searched Concord and burned what they found. Hancock and Adams escaped, however, and Pitcairn returned to Boston. Along the way, his men were harassed and ambushed almost continually by militiamen. By the time the English made it back to Boston, the War for American Independence was underway. The English claimed victory at Lexington, yet the Americans claimed victory at Concord.

Past, Present and Future — Although no one knows who fired the first "shot that was heard around the world", God does. In his providence, the American nation was born and it all started with that sovereign shot. John Jay, the first Chief Justice of the Supreme Court, claimed that providence "has given to our people the choice of their rulers". How do you see God's involvement in American affairs today?

Fort Ticonderoga

After the English returned to Boston, the American Colonists pursued them and surrounded the city, and the militia was put under the command of Artemus Ward, a French and Indian War veteran.

In order to set Boston under siege, the Colonists needed cannons, so Ethan Allen and Benedict Arnold volunteered to march north to Fort Ticonderoga on Lake Champlain to capture the cannons there.

The fort fell quickly and almost without a fight. Only one Colonist was injured, and the fort was captured practically painlessly. The guns were taken back to Boston by Henry Knox, a Bostonian patriot. When he returned, the Colonists were able to finally besiege General Gage in Boston.

Breed's Hill

Before Knox arrived with the artillery from Ticonderoga, the Americans had fought a fierce battle on Breed's Hill, near Boston. Many today call this the Battle of Bunker Hill, but that is a misunderstanding. Actually the names of two hills were switched around somehow, and the Americans thought they were fighting on Bunker Hill. The Battle of Bunker Hill became the accepted name of the conflict even though it was fought on Breed's Hill.

General Gage, in an attempt to drive the Colonists from the hill, sent William Howe to attack the rebel positions. Keep in mind, however, that the rebels had little ammunition because Henry Knox had not yet returned from Ticonderoga. William Prescott, a Colonial commander, ordered his men to "hold their fire until you see the whites of their eyes," meaning that the rebels were to conserve ammunition.

The Colonists took Prescott's advice and used their ammunition well. Despite being low on ammunition, the rebels killed and wounded many British troops. It became known as one of the most costly battles in the war for England. As a result, the Americans claimed victory, despite abandoning the hill.

When Knox returned with the artillery, the British, seeing their predicament, abandoned Boston.

THE BATTLE OF BUNKER HILL

Thinking More About It — Which side benefited most from the Battle of Breed's Hill?

The Declaration of Independence

Although battles had been fought in the war up to this point, the English, and many Colonists, still considered the conflict to be a colonial insurrection, a simple rebellion. But in July 1776, the Second Continental Congress did something that turned this insurrection into a full-swing revolution. They crossed the point of no return, so to speak, by declaring their independence from England. A committee of men, including Thomas Jefferson, Benjamin Franklin, John Adams, Robert Livingston and Roger Sherman, was put together to write the document that would change American history. Thomas Jefferson was chosen to actually write the document, and in July it was finished. The Declaration was voted for on the 2nd and adopted on the 4th. Today we celebrate July 4th as the birthday of our country, but John Adams thought that July 2nd would be hailed by later generations as the country's birthday. 56 members of the Continental Congress signed the Declaration of Independence throughout the summer. Let's make one thing clear, however. John Hancock did NOT sign his name like he did for King George to read without his spectacles as folklore would have us believe. Rather, he most likely signed his name this way because he was the President of the Continental Congress, and he himself was a type of man who probably signed his name like that most of the time. Also, although the signers never did sign the declaration all together, signer William Ellery claims they did. Historians are still unsure as to the plausibility of Ellery's claim.

Cool Fact

While writing the Declaration, Jefferson played his fiddle to clear his mind when he faced writer's block.

The Fall of New York

After the signing of the Declaration of Independence, the war became an official revolution, no longer just an insurrection by farmers and villagers against King George's rule.

George Washington was given command of the Continental Army, and he set to training his new army. Many were farmers and their sons, and they knew little of soldiery and almost nothing of the discipline it took to be an army. Many left when they felt like it, and others fought with men from rival colonies.

The early campaigns of the war were hard on the Colonists. The British beat them at New York. The Patriots were able to escape from Long Island under the cover of nightfall, but New York did fall to the British. Interestingly enough, the only man who saw the Patriots crossing was a slave to a Loyalist. He tried to warn the British but the only British guards around were Hessians from Germany fighting for England. They did not know English, and so they did not understand the slave's alert. Washington and his men were able to escape because of this. Many would call it a stroke of luck but it was, indeed, the Providence of God.

After what is called the Battle of Long Island, the Colonists were beaten again at the Battle of White Plains, nearby. However, Washington, once again, escaped under the cover of darkness.

Washington retreated into New Jersey after the fall of Fort Washington in New York.

Trenton and Princeton

After such defeats as those in New York, Washington desperately needed a victory to raise morale. Many of his men planned on going home at the end of 1776, and he had to convince them to stay.

On Christmas night, 1776, Washington led his troops across the Delaware River toward Trenton. The Hessians (Germans) were asleep in their barracks, so when Washington rushed into Trenton they didn't stand a chance. Washington beat the Germans badly that night, and the hopes of the American Revolution did not die.

One of the Colonists, Colonel John Fitzgerald told the story of Trenton in these words.

"It is a glorious victory. It will rejoice the hearts of our friends everywhere and give new life to our hitherto waning fortunes. Washington has...pounced upon the Hessians like an eagle upon a hen".

After the battle of Trenton, British General Lord Cornwallis decided to attack Washington. However, his men were defeated at Princeton nearby and the attack failed. Washington waited out the winter in New Jersey as more and more men streamed in to the join the cause of liberty.

The Capture of Philadelphia

In 1777, British General Howe marched his army into Pennsylvania to capture the colonial capital Philadelphia. On September 11, 1777, the British and Americans clashed at Brandywine Creek. Eventually the British won the battle and quickly occupied Philadelphia within weeks. Washington finally gave up after being defeated outside the city at Germantown in early October.

Although the loss of Philadelphia was terrible for the Colonists, they were able to turn the tide in the coming weeks.

The Battles of Bennington, Bemis Heights and Saratoga

The British were also attacking the Americans from Canada. They sent a young commander named John Burgoyne down to attack New England. John Burgoyne was called Gentleman Johnny because of his attractiveness and good looks. He may have been handsome, but he was not very smart in the ways of war. Some colonial fighters dressed as civilians approached his army at Bennington in modern Vermont. Burgoyne assumed they were Loyalists. They attacked his forces suddenly and dealt them a decisive blow. Burgoyne rashly attacked more Americans at Bemis Heights and again was defeated.

GENERAL BURGOYNE SURRENDERS TO GENERAL
GATES AT SARATOGA

The final battle in the campaign came on October 17, 1777, at Saratoga, New York. Burgoyne was completely defeated, and he was forced to surrender. The British plan to invade from the north had failed and the Americans saw this as a great victory. Not only that, but, the French also realized that the hopes of the revolution were not lost. Benjamin Franklin had been over in France for most of the war, pleading with the French king to side with the Americans and aid them in their revolution. The French king refused because he did not think the Americans could win. After Saratoga, however, he changed his mind and France joined the Americans against the English.

The Battle of Monmouth Courthouse and the Treason of Benedict Arnold

In June 1778, the British and American forces met again in a major battle at Monmouth Courthouse in New Jersey. During the battle, Henry Lee, an American commander, called a retreat. Washington was so upset that he fired Lee on the spot. This battle proved inconclusive and the British retreated under the cover of night. The Americans had won at Saratoga, but the British made it clear that they were not giving up yet.

The British had a powerful weapon on their side. Benedict Arnold, who had been an important colonial commander. He had secretly been spying for the British. He had fallen in love with a Loyalist and she had turned him against the Americans. His disloyalty can also be owed to the fact that he had been demoted and had not received the promotions and positions that he thought he deserved.

Arnold and some British officers plotted to take over West Point, an influential American fort. Although the plan failed, Arnold escaped and became a commander in the British army.

Thinking More About It — What might have happened if the surrender of West Point had been successful?

The War in the South

Throughout the early years of the war, the British and Americans had mostly fought on Northern ground. Battles had raged across New England and the Mid-Atlantic States, like Pennsylvania, Maryland and Delaware.

In 1778, the British decided to invade the Southern states, Virginia, North and South Carolina and Georgia. In November, the British commander Colonel Campbell invaded Georgia. In December he defeated the Americans at Savannah and later at Augusta, gaining control of Georgia. The British then invaded South Carolina. They besieged the city of Charleston. Eventually in the spring of 1779, the city surrendered.

The next battle went down in American history with a rotten record. The Battle of Camden was perhaps the most notorious battle of the American Revolution. There, the Americans were defeated terribly by the British under Banastre Tarleton. After the battle, Tarleton ordered that all the American prisoners were to be killed. This resulted in great hatred for Tarleton and wishes for revenge.

Those wishes were granted in October 1780. By then the British had invaded North Carolina. Major Patrick Ferguson led the British to camp on King's Mountain on the border between North and South Carolina. The Americans attacked and soundly defeated the British and killed Ferguson. Another American victory followed at Cowpens in South Carolina, in which Tarleton was defeated, yet he escaped.

At Guilford Courthouse in North Carolina, the Americans were able to fend off the British, and Cornwallis, the British commander, decided to invade Virginia. It was during this campaign that the final major battle would be fought.

> **Cool Fact**
>
> Francis Marion, the "Swamp Fox," outwitted the British by leading his men through the swamps of South Carolina as the Redcoats pursued him. They couldn't catch him!

The Battle of Yorktown

It was during the campaign in Virginia that the Battle of Yorktown was fought in September 1781.

Cornwallis set up his camp at Yorktown on the Virginia coast. Washington and a Frenchman named Jean-Baptiste Donatien de Vimeur, Comte de Rochambeau led the American army to Yorktown. Meanwhile, the French admiral de Grasse was heading there with a French fleet of ships.

Because the French controlled the sea, Cornwallis could not escape or receive help. The Americans and French outnumbered him and eventually Cornwallis surrendered October 19, 1781.

Although the war did not officially end until 1783 at the Treaty of Paris, the Battle of Yorktown was the last large battle of the war. By then, the Americans had proven that they were capable of winning, and they had practically gained their independence. It was only a matter of time before this independence became official. The first nation to recognize American independence was the Netherlands.

The United States of America was born.

Thinking More About It — Why do you think the French supported the Americans during the war?

The Beginnings of American Government

After the Colonists had achieved their independence from Britain, they set about the task of organizing a new nation.

The Founding Fathers wanted to set up a republic. A republic is a representative government ruled by the law rather than by a certain person or group of persons. The American founders didn't want to create a democracy. Democracy is the rule of the majority. The founders hated this idea and recognized it as dangerous and deadly.

Although the idea of the Republic was not necessarily new, it had not been enacted before. The American Republic was the first in the world and therefore, there were some issues that faced the first American statesmen.

Many smaller states wanted to have a strong central government with equal representation for all the states. The larger states wanted to have the power stay in the state's hands and they wanted larger states to have more power than smaller ones. Things had to be worked out quickly.

The states worked like a group of individuals rather than a team. The states wanted to be loosely connected to each other but to be practically independent. The early United States was having problems working together. In fact, George Washington had to lead the U.S. army to put down the Whiskey Rebellion in 1791 in Western Pennsylvania. The farmers of this area were rebelling against a tax levied on whiskey by Secretary of the Treasury Alexander Hamilton.

You can see that a lot of issues faced the new nation; a constitution was desperately needed. James Madison, a Founding Father from Virginia, was the one to write most of the Constitution and thus earned the title "Father of the Constitution." He, along with John Jay and Alexander Hamilton, penned a series of essays now known as the Federalist Papers. These essays were like a commentary on the Constitution.

As to the question of state's rights, the American government was set up so that a compromise was reached. Two houses were created in the Congress, the House of Representatives and the Senate. The Senate was made up of two senators from each state so that the smaller states that wanted equal power were pleased.

The House of Representatives was made up of delegates from different states. The number of Representatives depended on the population of the state, thereby pleasing the larger states that wanted greater power based on population.

Some people wanted George Washington to be king, but George and many others disagreed. Hadn't they just rebelled against a King George? Instead George was elected America's first president. Immediately, problems were thrown on him, from both inside and outside the country.

Thinking More About It — Why did George Washington refuse to become King?

Cool Fact

The American Founding Fathers based their political philosophy on Christian doctrines. Even the idea of checks and balances, originally philosophized by French thinker Montesquieu, was based on Isaiah 33:22, "The LORD is our Judge (judicial), the LORD is our lawgiver (legislative) and the LORD is our King (executive). He will save us." Samuel Adams declared that "We have this day restored the Sovereign to whom all men must be obedient. He reigns in Heaven, and from the rising to the setting of the sun, let his Kingdom come!"

CHAPTER THREE

AMERICA FIGHTS TO STAY FREE

The French Revolution

In 1794, the Bourbon King of France, Louis XVI, who had sent French troops to America during the Revolution, was deposed and killed by French revolutionaries. These French patriots had seen the success of the Americans in throwing down their own authority and so had begun their own revolution against their own king. What followed was called the "Reign of Terror" because of the great violence in the streets. Hundreds of people suspected of being "anti-Revolutionary" were executed. Many people in America thought that the new nation should assist the French revolutionaries because the French had supported the American revolutionaries.

Although the United States did not get involved, the British did. They also concluded a treaty with the Americans. The French were outraged that the Americans would make a treaty with the British who were "anti-revolutionaries." They broke diplomatic relations with America and battles were even fought on the high seas between the fleets of United States and France. During John Adams' term as President (1797-1801), several French agents tried to bribe the United States into supporting the French and restoring diplomatic relations. This is now known as the XYZ Affair and the entire conflict between the United States and France is known as the "Quasi War" (quasi means "almost"). In 1800, a convention between the two countries was signed, officially ending the strife.

Barbary Pirates

Meanwhile, the Barbary pirates of North Africa had also been preying on the young country. The Barbary pirates came from the North African state of Tripoli. These Arab pirates usually raided American ships in the Mediterranean and enslaved the crews.

The United States was outraged and, in 1801, the American marines attacked Tripoli. Many of the battles were naval battles fought off the coast of North Africa, but eventually the Americans, along with Greek, Arab and Swedish allies, invaded Tripoli itself and won a decisive battle at Derne. There the Americans raised their flag on foreign ground for the first time. This became eternally commemorated with the line "to the shores of Tripoli" in the official song of the U.S. Marines. During this first war with Tripoli, a young naval commander went on one of the most famous missions in U.S. naval history. Stephen Decatur, a young American naval commander, was commissioned to blow up a captured American ship called the Philadelphia in Tripoli harbor. He did this secretly and succeeded in blowing up the ship and keeping the Barbary pirates from capturing the ammunition and supplies held on the ship.

THE USS PHILADELPHIA BURSTS INTO FLAME IN TRIPOLI HARBOR

British admiral Horatio Gates called it the "most bold and daring act of the age". By 1805, Tripoli wanted peace so the first official war against a foreign power was a victory for the United States. However, Algiers, another Barbary state, began preying on the U.S. merchant ships and so in 1815, the Second Barbary War was fought. The Americans also won this war, easily.

Causes of the War of 1812

Just as America had to fight to stay free from the pirating and plundering of the Tripolitans, they had to fight to stay free from oppression by Britain. The United States fought a major war with Britain between 1812 and 1815. This war is called the War of 1812.

The three main reasons for war between Great Britain and the United States were impressment, free trade and conflict with the Native Americans in the West.

Impressment—The British had been fighting a long war with Napoleonic France through the first decade of the 1800s. The French navy had threatened the British dominion of the High Seas. To combat this, the British had been building their navy and, starting in 1807, had begun to kidnap American sailors to sail their new ships and fight for them. The Americans were enraged that the British would be so brazen. Many American sailors fell into slavery-like service in the British navy between 1807 and 1812.

Free Trade—The British had also been blockading the European continent to fight against the French economy.

They refused to let American merchant ships into European waters. America was a neutral country in the war between France and Great Britain, and they argued that because of this they should have free trade with both France and Great Britain. President Thomas Jefferson enacted an embargo (trade restriction) on France and Great Britain in 1807, but this proved to hurt the United States more than it did Great Britain.

Native American Conflicts—Although we will later explore the westward expansion of the United States, let us now simply say that America had taken control of all the territory from the Atlantic Ocean in the East to Oregon in the West. Although early settlers had lived relatively peaceably with the Native Americans, the more settlers that came, the more tensions rose. One Native American leader named Tecumseh attempted to unite the Native American nations of the Ohio-Indiana-Michigan area. This great Native American nation built a fortress at Prophetstown, in Indiana. In 1811, William Henry Harrison, the governor of Indiana, took an army of American troops out toward Prophetstown on the Tippecanoe River. The Native Americans attacked the American camp at night, and the costly battle of Tippecanoe was fought, ending inconclusively. Later, Harrison led his men to Prophetstown and destroyed it. During the destruction of Prophetstown, Harrison's men found British muskets in the fort. The British had been keeping peace with the Native Americans by giving them guns and ammunition. The Americans thought that Great Britain was trying to stir the Native Americans against them.

For these reasons, President James Madison declared war on Great Britain in June of 1812.

Thinking More About It — What do you think was the most important cause of the War of 1812?

The First Invasion of Canada

The American war plan against the British was to invade Canada and take control of the Great Lakes. This would be a major front of the war, and much fighting took place in Canada and the present states of Michigan, Ohio, Indiana, Illinois and New York.

The first invasion of Canada began in 1812 with Revolutionary War veteran William Hull leading the main attack. Hull marched his army to Fort Detroit (present Detroit) and crossed the Detroit River to the town of Sandwich, Canada. The Americans took Sandwich but retreated across the river when they heard that Fort Michilimackinac had fallen to the British and that British reinforcements were marching from Fort Malden. Meanwhile, the British had taken Fort Dearborn (present Chicago), and Isaac Brock, the British general in Upper Canada, was marching his men towards Fort Detroit with his Native American allies under Tecumseh. When the British began to bombard Fort Detroit, Hull surrendered the fort to protect the civilians inside. The first invasion of Canada had succeeded only in giving up three forts to the British.

War at Sea

Although the American invasion of Canada had failed, General Hull's nephew Isaac had better success on the High Seas.

Isaac Hull's ship, the USS Constitution, met the British ship HMS Guerriere in battle in the Atlantic Ocean. During the battle a cannonball bounced off the side of the Constitution, leading to the iconic term "Old Ironsides." Eventually, the British captain surrendered his ship, and it was burned after being emptied of men and supplies.

Captain Stephen Decatur also won a great victory off the coast of the Azore Islands near Spain. His ship, the United States, defeated and destroyed the British ship Macedonian. Decatur hauled his prize, the captured ship, all the way across the Atlantic to New London, Connecticut, to show it off.

In 1813, Captain James Lawrence of the Hornet defeated the British ships Resolution and Peacock. The small American ship Essex preyed on British merchant ships in the Pacific, weakening the British economy. Other sea battles were fought on the Great Lakes. In 1813, the British blockaded and raided the Atlantic coast, also weakening the American economy.

The Battle of Queenston

The Americans were now plotting a second invasion of Canada. This time they would be attacking from Buffalo, New York. The American generals Smyth and Van Rensselaer disagreed on where to attack. Eventually, Van Rensselaer sent

Lieutenant Colonel Winfield Scott with some men to attack the Canadian village of Queenston. The Americans were able to take the town, but they surrendered when reinforcements arrived under Isaac Brock. Brock himself was killed in the fighting. After the failure of the invasion, General Henry Dearborn replaced Van Rensselaer with Smyth.

The Battles of the Raisin, York, Fort Meigs and Sackets Harbor

After the failure of William Hull's invasion at Detroit, he was replaced by the governor of the Indiana Territory, William Henry Harrison. Harrison ordered his men to build a fort on the Maumee River near Lake Erie in what is now northern Ohio. They called it Fort Meigs. As they built the fort, a dispatch went east to Frenchtown on the Raisin River in New York to defend the town against British attack. The British attacked under Lieutenant Colonel Henry Proctor. The Americans fled and many were killed by Native Americans. The rest were taken prisoner. Late one night, the Native Americans massacred the Americans in the village, leading to the rise of the rally cry "Remember the Raisin" among the Americans.

The Americans attacked Canada again in the spring of 1813. They aimed their main strike at York (present Toronto). The army was led by Brigadier General Zebulon Pike, and the navy was led by Commodore Isaac Chauncey. Chauncey cleared Lake Ontario after positioning his forces at Sackets Harbor, New York. Pike then led his troops to capture York. The British knew that they could not hold out long against Pike's attack, so they set fire to the magazine (gun powder) in the fort and fled. When the Americans charged the fort, the magazine exploded, killing many of them, including Zebulon Pike. The Americans took the supplies and ammunition from the fort and returned to Sackets Harbor.

Meanwhile, the British under General Proctor attacked Fort Meigs. Harrison waited for reinforcements from Kentucky. The Kentucky frontiersmen showed up, scattering the British and Native Americans. However, they were lured away from the fort. Many were captured and later massacred. Tecumseh finally arrived, and ordered an end to the killing. He blamed Proctor for not stopping the massacre and not controlling the Native Americans. Although this was a hard time for the Americans, they succeeded in fending off the British siege and defending Fort Meigs. In May 1813, the Americans attacked Canada across the Niagara River at Fort George. They captured the fort and controlled both sides of the river after much fighting. Meanwhile, Sir George Prevost led British troops to attack Sackets Harbor. However, the attack failed when Jacob Brown's American troops fired upon the attacking British.

Prevost retreated and the Americans were victorious at Sackets Harbor.

The Lake Erie Campaign

The Americans decided to launch another attack on Canada in late 1813, centered around Lake Erie. First, however, the American navy had to clear the lake of British vessels. The American Lake Erie fleet was put under the command of Oliver Hazard Perry to do just that. The

American and British fleets clashed on Lake Erie in September. The British pounded Perry's flagship Lawrence and badly damaged it, but Perry refused to surrender. In the midst of the battle, he took his flag to another ship called the Niagara and continued the battle from that ship. The Americans won the battle and captured the entire British fleet. Perry sent a note to General William Henry Harrison saying, "We have met the enemy and they are ours."

The victory on Lake Erie enabled Harrison to march on Fort Malden to seize Detroit. When the Americans reached Fort Malden, they found the fort abandoned by the British who had retreated with Tecumseh's forces.

General Proctor arranged his men in a marsh along the Thames River. The American advance guard under Richard Johnson charged the British and Proctor fled. The Americans then turned on the Native Americans under Tecumseh. In the battle that ensued, the great Native American leader was killed and with him died the hopes of uniting the Northwest Native American nations.

The Battle of the Thames enabled the Americans to seize control of Illinois, Indiana, Michigan, and Wisconsin.

The Americans had successfully driven the British out of the Lake Erie territory, but an attempt to invade Montreal failed because of poor communication between cooperating officers.

The final engagements of the Lake Erie campaign were fought around Buffalo, New York, where British and American forces burned and ravaged the enemy's towns.

The Creek War

Before his death, Tecumseh had gone south to Mississippi to appeal to the Creek nation to join his Native American alliance. The Creek elders refused, but a group of young fanatics, who called themselves the "Red Sticks" after their war clubs, left the Creek nation and massacred American settlers at Fort Mims on the Tallapoosa River in what is now Alabama, near Pensacola, Florida. The Creek elders tracked down the young killers and killed them in turn. This resulted in all the Creek Red Sticks rising up against the Creek nation and the United States.

General Andrew Jackson was sent south to Mississippi to deal with the Red Stick threat. His army of 3,000 Americans set out from Fort Strother in Northern Alabama with a few hundred Native American allies, including Cherokee and Creek.

They attacked the Red Sticks at Horseshoe Bend on the Tallapoosa River in Alabama, near the Alabama-Georgia border. At first, the battle went badly for the Americans. They were unable to capture the Red Stick fort. However, the Cherokee and Creek allies sent some men across the river behind the fort to steal the Red Sticks' escape canoes and set fire to the fort. They then sent their entire force to the rear of the fort. Finally after a long battle, the Red Sticks were defeated.

After the Creek War, Jackson and his army stayed in the Southern territories of Mississippi and Louisiana.

Cool Fact

The Cherokee leader at Horseshoe Bend saved Jackson's life after the battle from a sneaking Creek warrior. Years later, when Jackson exiled the Cherokee people from their land, the Cherokee chief regretted his actions. He admitted that if he had known what would come, he would he have let Jackson die.

The Final Niagara Campaign

In July 1814, the American army under Jacob Brown invaded Canada one last time from Buffalo, New York. The Americans crossed the Niagara River toward Fort Erie. The Americans captured the fort and continued to march north. They met the British at Chippewa where the two armies faced each other, European style--in neat formations on an open plain. The Americans successfully drove the British back, proving that they could defeat British forces in open battle.

American and British forces once again engaged each other at Lundy's Lane at night in late July. The battle raged through the night as American troops assaulted the British who were entrenched on a hill. Eventually, the Americans took the hill and claimed victory, but the victory did not give the Americans any major advantage over the British.

The British then turned to attack Fort Erie, but they failed to do so. The last invasion of Canada had ended in a practical stalemate.

The Maryland Campaign

The British decided to launch an attack on the American Atlantic coast to gain an advantage before peace talks began. The Russians had begun to offer peace talks between Great Britain and the United States, but the British wanted to invade the U.S. coast before they began to settle the war once and for all.

The British had been raiding the U.S. coast throughout the year of 1813 and once again attacked in Spring 1814.

In August, the British landed in Maryland, about 30 miles from Washington, D.C. The British under General Robert Ross marched along the Patuxent River. Then they marched north to the Anacostia River where they crossed at Bladensburg, Maryland.

The Americans at Bladensburg held fast for a while but soon retreated when the British bombarded their positions with Congreve Rockets—a new military weapon that was much like a mortar. It made a screaming sound as it flew. The Battle of the Bladensburg Races was a British victory because it enabled them to march unopposed into Washington, D.C.

When the Americans heard that the British were marching on Washington, many fled. These included the President James Madison and his wife Dolley, who first rescued a portrait of George Washington and a copy of the

Declaration of Independence among other important papers from the White House. When the British entered the capital, they set fire to many buildings including the White House and the Capitol.

The Battle of Lake Champlain

While the British were invading Maryland, they were also busy attacking from Montreal in the north. In September, British troops invaded New York. Thomas MacDonough positioned the American fleet at Lake Champlain while the American army readied itself at Plattsburgh, New York.

When the British fleet entered Lake Champlain, a large battle ensued between the two navies. Eventually, the Americans emerged victorious.

Because of the American victory on Lake Champlain, the British retreated from Plattsburgh.

The Battle of Baltimore

The British turned from Washington, D.C., to attack Baltimore, which they described as a "nest of pirates."

The fort guarding Baltimore was called Fort McHenry. The British fleet bombarded the fort all day and all night but eventually were forced to pull away. When Francis Scott Key, a lawyer, saw the American flag still flying high above Fort McHenry, he penned a poem called "The Star-Spangled Banner", which later became America's national anthem.

THE BATTLE OF NEW ORLEANS

The Battle of New Orleans

The British attempted to win one more battle against the Americans before peace was made. They decided to strike at New Orleans where Andrew Jackson's army was stationed. The British under General Edward Packenham attacked. The Americans were hidden behind low walls made of dirt and earth called breastworks. The Americans fired again and again at the charging British. The British were forced to fall back. Actually, the battle was fought a couple of weeks after the peace treaty, but the news of the treaty had not yet reached New Orleans. Jackson's great victory at New Orleans not only ended the war but also ended British domination in North America.

In 1823, President James Monroe established the Monroe Doctrine, which forbid any European power from entangling itself in the affairs of the Americans. Europeans could no longer establish colonies in North and South America, and American independence was set in stone, once and for all. The United States then entered into a period of isolation in which it was not involved in world affairs.

Cool Fact

The Americans lost fewer than twenty men, killed and wounded in the Battle of New Orleans. The British lost hundreds.

The Treaty of Ghent

In 1814, the Treaty of Ghent, named for a town in what is now Belgium, officially ended the War of 1812. Neither side emerged significantly victorious, but the Americans were able to preserve their liberty.

CHAPTER FOUR

U.S. EXPANSION

The Louisiana Purchase

In 1783, when the United States was officially recognized as an independent country, its borders extended from the Atlantic Ocean to the east bank of the Mississippi River and from Maine in the north to Georgia in the south. The modern-day states of Kentucky, Ohio, Tennessee and Indiana were considered the "Western Frontier." However, many Americans soon realized that in order for the country to thrive it had to grow larger. In those days, the United States was surrounded by colonies of other European empires. Great Britain owned Canada, and the Spanish controlled Florida and everything west of the Mississippi. Originally the French had controlled the land west of the Mississippi called Louisiana, but they had "given" it to the Spanish after the French and Indian War.

You see, the French feared that the British would take Louisiana from them in the peace treaty. (It was customary for the winner of a war to take territory from the loser.) The French did not want Louisiana to fall into British hands so they "gave" it to Spain. How generous of them. The British could do nothing about it.

So, in 1800 Spain still held on to Louisiana and the port of New Orleans that controlled the Mississippi.

The United States had limited and, at most times, unreliable access to New Orleans. Sometimes the Spanish would not let the American tradesmen bring their goods into the city. The United States desperately wanted control of the Mississippi but things were complicated in 1800.

In 1800, the dictator of France, Napoleon Bonaparte, made a treaty with Spain at San Ildefonso. In the treaty, Napoleon agreed to let the Spanish duke of Parma (in Italy) take over the Kingdom of Etruria (in Italy) if he could get Louisiana back. However, he decided to change to deal before Charles IV of Spain signed the treaty. Rather than the Duke of Parma, Napoleon wanted the duke's son, Louis, to rule Etruria. He also wanted Florida from Spain.

King Charles agreed to make Louis the ruler of Etruria but refused Florida. The king and the dictator squabbled about the terms of the treaty for a long time, and the King of Spain did not sign the treaty for a few years. Meanwhile, in good hope that the treaty would go through, Napoleon sent his brother-in-law, General Leclerc, to retake the island of Hispaniola (now the Dominican Republic and Haiti). A slave revolt led by Toussaint L'Overture had overthrown the French settler's government in the colony of Santo Domingo on the island in 1795.

Leclerc took a large expedition to retake the island from the rebels. At first, he was able to make some headway and even tricked L'Overture into surrendering. But the Santo Dominicans found new leaders and drove the French away, killing Leclerc in the process.

Napoleon realized that Louisiana was worthless without Hispaniola under his control. Hispaniola was the most lucrative French colony in North America and would be the supply base for his army in Louisiana.

Meanwhile, the Americans were desperately trying to stop the Treaty of San Ildefonso from going through. They were sure that Napoleon would attack their nation if he got hold of Louisiana. They appealed to Great Britain for help and even threatened to declare war on France if the deal went through. The British supported them because they themselves were at war with France. President Thomas Jefferson, ordered Robert Livingston, an American minister to France to offer to buy Louisiana from the French.

Surprisingly, the French minister Talleyrand offered to sell Louisiana to the Americans first.

While these negotiations were going on in France, the Spanish customs officer in New Orleans had closed the port to American goods. However, Charles IV of Spain soon forced him to reopen the port. Eventually, Talleyrand and Napoleon agreed to sell Louisiana to the United States for 15 million U.S. dollars—about 4 cents per acre. When Charles IV signed the treaty of San Ildefonso, the French seized control of Louisiana and within weeks gave it over to the Americans.

The only thing that stood in the way of America's annexation of Louisiana was the U.S. Constitution.

A map of the Louisiana Purchase

The Constitution had made no provision for expanding American territory. The Congress was divided on whether to accept the Louisiana Purchase. Eventually, Congress recognized the treaty, but it remained controversial for some time.

By 1803, the United States had annexed the Louisiana Territory, which stretched from New Orleans on the Mississippi River to the region that is now the state of Montana.

Thinking More About It — Why do you think Napoleon decided to sell Louisiana to the Americans?

The Lewis and Clark Expedition

The Louisiana Territory was largely unknown to the Americans, even those along the Mississippi frontier. Thomas Jefferson sent two former army captains, Merriweather Lewis and William Clark, on an expedition with some fifty men to explore the vast land. With the Native American guide Sacajawea leading them and accompanied by Sacajawea's Canadian husband, they journeyed through the vast wilderness to the Pacific Ocean. After waiting awhile for a ship to bring them back to the eastern United States, they set off again across land, not knowing that the British ship Lydia would arrive on the Pacific coast in just 19 days.

LEWIS AND CLARK EMBARK ON THEIR EXPEDITION

Soon settlers began to drift into the territory and then began to pour in. They were driven by an ideology called "Manifest Destiny," which claimed that God had destined America to spread "from sea to shining sea" and that it was America's duty to God to subdue the Native American populations and build a nation that would dominate the continent.

Many settlers did clash with the Native Americans as they drove westward, and eventually President Andrew Jackson forced the Creek nation out of its homeland in Mississippi-Alabama. Thousands of Creek and other Native American nations, including the Cherokee, were exiled westward. They emigrated along the "Trail of Tears." Continued conflict with Native Americans would drag on until the 1890s.

Florida Cession

Meanwhile, the United States had its eyes set on Spanish Florida. Even before the Louisiana Purchase of 1803, the Americans had been looking to acquire Florida, but the Spanish were not willing to part with it.

Forts in northern Florida had been built by escaped slaves from the United States and some of these freemen frequently raided American soil. The Americans used this as an excuse to invade Florida multiple times between 1810 to 1818. The largest invasion occurred under future president Andrew Jackson in 1819. Jackson led his men into Florida to punish the Seminole nation of Native Americans for their raids. The Spanish objected but were eventually forced to cede Florida and a small portion of Colorado to the United States in the Adams-Onis Treaty of 1819.

The Mexican-American War

By the 1840s, the United States stretched from the Atlantic Coast to the Rockies. (The Oregon Territory, which now comprises the states of Oregon, Washington, and Idaho, had not been officially acquired yet; it was still a disputed region with the British.) Mexico, which had gained its independence from Spain in 1821, controlled the Southwest, now the states of California, Nevada, Arizona, New Mexico, Texas, Oklahoma, Colorado, and Utah. The United States looked to gain this territory and attempted to buy it from Mexico. But the Mexicans said that it was not for sale.

At about the same time, the Texans, mostly American settlers who had settled in Mexican territory, were waging a war of independence against Mexico. The Mexican army under Antonio de Santa Anna defeated them at the battle of The Alamo, taking no prisoners but killing the fort's entire garrison. Not long after, Sam Houston led the Texans in victory over the Mexicans at the battle of San Jacinto in 1836 and declared the independence of the Texas Republic.

In 1845, Texas was admitted to the United States. It had not been admitted upon its independence. It was a slave state, and the government was reluctant to welcome it to the Union.

In 1846, President James K. Polk sent the American army to the Texas-Mexico border. American and Mexican troops exchanged fire near Brownsville, Texas, and the Mexican-American War had begun.

The Americans quickly defeated the Mexicans at the battle of Palo Alto and Monterrey, Mexico. Meanwhile, California had declared its independence from Mexico. The U.S. navy seized Monterey, California, soon afterwards.

General Zachary Taylor defeated the Mexicans at Buena Vista in early 1847. General Winfield Scott landed his troops at Veracruz, Mexico. Soon, Scott's army was marching on Mexico City. They defeated the Mexicans at Cerro Gordo and went on to capture Mexico City itself. The final fight was at the Mexican military academy at Fort Chapultepec in 1848.

The Treaty of Guadalupe-Hidalgo was signed in 1848, ending the war. The Americans forced Mexico to cede its entire empire north of the Rio Grande river to the United States. This did not include a small portion of southern New Mexico and southern Arizona. This territory was later purchased in 1853 in what is called the Gadsden Purchase.

Thinking More About It — Was the American war against Mexico a justified fight for liberty or a greedy land-grab? Discuss.

Canadian-American Boundaries

Ever since the War of 1812, the British and Americans had maintained some uncertainties about the border between the United States and British North America (Canada).

In 1818, the British and Americans signed a treaty that gave the United States significant gains in northwestern Minnesota and northeastern North Dakota. The treaty set the border at the 49th Parallel. However, the two nations still disagreed over Oregon. In 1846, Britain and the United States signed another treaty recognizing America's claim on the Oregon Territory.

The Homestead Act

In 1862, the United States government passed the Homestead Act, which gave Americans the right to claim land in the West and settle it. This, and the discovery of gold in California in 1849, quickly populated the West. This brought about the age of boom towns. It also brought settlers in conflict with Native Americans.

CHAPTER FIVE

THE SLAVERY DEBATE

Nothing divided the United States during these early years more than slavery. Many people in the North (New England, the Mid-Atlantic states) believed that slavery was wrong, but many people in the South (the Southeast and Deep South states) relied on slavery to run their plantations. In fact, the Southern economy depended on slave labor. This issue of whether to allow slavery in the land of the free divided the nation in a very visible way.

The debate over slavery was heated. Congress worked for decades to come to a conclusion, and for decades Congressmen expressed angry words over the issue. Slowly, some gains were made and some steps taken toward decisive legislation, but these steps enraged some and embittered the two sides against each other.

At the heart of the slavery issue was the issue of States' Rights and whether states could choose for themselves whether to allow slavery. Also, the question of states entering the Union was brought up. Who would decide if these new states would be pro-slavery (Slave States) or anti-slavery (Free States)? And what if a slave owner from a Slave State moved with his slaves to a Free State? Would they become free? As American territory expanded so did the intensity of the debate over slavery.

Past, Present, Future — What issues divide Americans nowadays?

The Missouri Compromise

In 1808, Congress had outlawed the import of slaves from Africa, but there were still many slaves in the United States. They had children, so the legislation did not have a great effect on the slave population—or the slavery issue.

The first compromise between the two sides of the slavery issue came in 1820. It was then that the two sides came to an agreement called the Missouri Compromise. This legislation abolished slavery in the Louisiana Territory north of the 36°30' Parallel Latitude. This line runs along the southern border of the states of Virginia, Kentucky, and Missouri. Although these states (most importantly Missouri) were north of the 36°30' Parallel, they stayed Slave States. All other states south of the line were Slave States. With the exception of Virginia, Kentucky and Missouri, all states north of the line were Free States. Missouri was admitted into the Union as a Slave State and Maine as a Free State, and the balance of power was maintained. Most everyone was happy. Except, of course, for the slaves south of the Missouri Compromise latitude and a few cantankerous lawmakers who were still not satisfied.

The Compromise of 1850

In 1850, another compromise occurred between the two factions. California was admitted to the Union as a Free State, and Utah and New Mexico became territories that could choose by "popular sovereignty" whether to allow slavery. Popular sovereignty was mainly the idea of Stephen A. Douglass, who ran for president against Abraham Lincoln and engaged with him in the famous Lincoln-Douglass debates.

The most controversial legislation that was passed during the Compromise of 1850 was the Fugitive Slave Act, which forced escaped slaves to be returned to their masters if they were caught in the North.

A SKIRMISH DURING THE BLEEDING KANSAS WAR

The Kansas-Nebraska Act and "Bleeding Kansas"

In 1854, Stephen Douglass pushed for a law called the Kansas-Nebraska Act, which repealed the Missouri Compromise of 1820. Kansas and Nebraska became U.S. territories and were granted the right to choose their own position on slavery by popular sovereignty. This resulted in hundreds of settlers pouring into Kansas to sway the plebiscite vote. They didn't just vote on the issue, though; they fought over it. In 1855, Free State and Slave State factions clashed in battles across Kansas. Eventually, the "war" called Bleeding Kansas was over after much fighting and looting and burning, with a Free State victory in 1859. In all, about 56 people died during the years of war in Kansas.

Meanwhile, back in Congress passionate words had erupted in violence. In 1856, U.S. Representative from South Carolina Preston Brooks attacked Charles Sumner, a Massachusetts Senator, with his cane, causing him to lapse into unconsciousness. When other Senators tried to break up the fight, a Senator Laurence Keitt waved his pistol in the air urging them to fight it out.

John Brown's Raid on Harper's Ferry

John Brown, a fervent abolitionist and one of the leaders of the Free State faction in Kansas, wanted to arm the slaves and start a slave revolt in Virginia. He decided to take a band of men and attack the U.S. arsenal at Harper's Ferry. Brown's party attacked on the night of October 16, 1859. Over the next couple of days, U.S. marines under Robert E. Lee stormed the armory, eventually capturing Brown who was later executed. Before his death, Brown prophesied that the issue of slavery would only result in more bloodshed and that all-out war would come. He was right.

Visit www.highpointhistoryseries.com/bonuses/ for FREE bonus videos.

PART TWO:
1861-1945

CHAPTER SIX

THE CIVIL WAR

Causes of the Civil War

The first thing that must be said about the causes of the Civil War is that there is still much debate and disagreement about the true nature of the causes. Some will say slavery, others say state's rights. I believe it is an issue of *state's rights concerning slavery.*

The issue of state's rights was as old as the nation itself. Before the Constitution was even written the founding fathers were faced with a dilemma. Some politicians argued that without a strong, central government the nation would fall apart. These men were called Federalists because they supported a strong Federal government. Prominent Federalists included Alexander Hamilton, John Jay and James Madison (the authors of the Federalist Papers). On the other hand, some wanted more power to be in the hands of the states. These men were known as Anti-Federalists. Prominent Anti-Federalists included Patrick Henry, Thomas Jefferson and Samuel Adams. The Anti-Federalists feared that the President would become an American version of the King of England.

The battle between Federalism and Anti-Federalism didn't end with the ratification of the Constitution however. Instead, the battle to see whether the federal or state governments would have more power continued, manifesting itself in the slavery debate. When a new state entered the Union, who would decide if slavery was legal in that state? The federal government or the state itself? This was the question that contributed so much to the beginning of the Civil War.

In the past, some decisions had been made concerning this issue but it was still a point of disagreement between legislators.

Now let's review some of the legislation that had been passed concerning slavery.

First, the Missouri Compromise, passed in 1820, set an imaginary line at the 36°30' longitude (along the southern border of Virginia, Kentucky and Missouri). North of this line, slavery was illegal, (with the exception of the states listed above and Maryland and Delaware). South of this line, slavery was legal. Also, Missouri was admitted to the Union as a slave state and Maine was admitted as a free state so as to maintain the balance between Pro-Slave and Anti-Slave factions in the Congress.

The Compromise of 1850 was passed, which was the first major legislation that introduced the idea of "popular sovereignty". Popular sovereignty encouraged states to decide their policy on slavery by holding plebiscite votes. A plebiscite vote is one in which all the voters decide on an issue directly rather than voting for representatives.

The Election of 1860

By 1860 the country was in turmoil. A book written by Hinton Rowan Helper, a North Carolinian who denounced slavery, had circulated through the country and stirred up a major crisis in the House of Representatives.

During the presidential election of 1860, there were four candidates. John Bell of the Constitutional Union party was a moderate and didn't directly address the issue of slavery. John Breckinridge was a pro-slavery Southern democrat who wanted government legal protection for slavery. Stephan Douglas was also a democrat who endorsed popular sovereignty. Abraham Lincoln was an Illinois republican who endorsed state's rights but disagreed with slavery.

Lincoln was elected and the South exploded in anger. Lincoln hadn't carried a single Southern state, (in fact, almost all Southern states were carried by Breckinridge). Actually Lincoln hadn't even been on the ballot in some Southern states. The South felt that its voice in the federal government was threatened and they resented the election of a Republican as President. They decided it was time to form their own nation.

Southern Secession

The first state to secede from the Union was South Carolina which withdrew from the Union in December 1860. South Carolina was followed by Mississippi, Florida, Alabama, Georgia, Louisiana and Texas. These states declared a confederacy: the Confederate States of America. They elected Jefferson Davis as their President and established their capital at Montgomery, Alabama. Confederate military forces began to seize Federal forts and military outposts. Outgoing President James Buchanan did little to stop them, saying that it was not the government's responsibility to keep states from secession.

In April 1861, Confederate troops attacked Fort Sumter in South Carolina. This incident caused President Lincoln, now inaugurated, to call for the army to mobilize. Lincoln's call to war caused four more states to secede: North Carolina, Virginia, Tennessee and Arkansas. The Confederate was moved soon after to Richmond, Virginia. Several slave states did not secede. These included Maryland, Delaware, Kentucky, Missouri and West Virginia (a secessionist region of Virginia which seceded from Virginia because of Virginia's secession from the Union.) These were called the Border states.

Cool Fact

Abraham Lincoln wanted Robert E. Lee to lead the Union armies to war against the Confederacy. At first Lee was willing but when Virginia seceded from the Union he refused, so as to stay loyal to his state. As many people know, Lee became one of the greatest Confederate generals. This is very telling of the high regard for state over country that some men had at the time.

Thinking More About It — Do you think the South justified in seceding?

Early Military Engagements

The first main military engagement between Union and Confederate ground forces occurred in June 1861 at Philippi in what is now West Virginia. The battle ended in victory for the Union. A week later another battle occurred in Virginia at Big Bethel. This battle could be described as the "Bunker Hill" of the Civil War. The Union forces attacked Confederate troops near a church and were repelled. This was the first major Confederate victory besides Fort Sumter's surrender. This battle proved, very much like the battle of

Bunker Hill during the American Revolution, that victory would not be easy and quick for the Union forces. In July the Confederates again defeated the Union at the First Battle of Manassas (also known as the First Battle of Bull Run). This defeat caused mild panic in the North. During this battle, Confederate General Thomas Jackson earned his iconic nickname "Stonewall". As he charged into the battle one of his fellow commanders cried out "There stands Jackson like a stone wall!".

Meanwhile, across the Mississippi River in Missouri, Confederate militias clashed with Union troops. The major battle on this front in the early stages of the war was the Battle of Wilson's Creek which ended in Confederate victory. Nathaniel Lyons, one of the Union generals was killed during the battle. Later the Union won at Pea Ridge, Arkansas, thus gaining predominant control over Missouri. Native American cavalry fought alongside the Confederates at Pea Ridge. Sporadic fighting would continue in the area and William Quantrill would later lead Confederate raiders in a notorious raid on Lawrence, Kansas in 1863.

> *Cool Fact*
>
> Many college football rivalries in the Midwest originated in the Civil War. The rivalry between the Kansas Jayhawks and Missouri Tigers originated from Quantrill's raid on Lawrence, Kansas. In fact, the term Jayhawk is a Civil War term. It refers to "Jayhawkers," armed men who supported abolition during Bleeding Kansas, a "civil war" in Kansas a couple of years before the War Between the States began.

The Trent Affair

Many issues faced the Confederacy during the early months of the Civil War. One of them was the lack of formal recognition from other countries. The Confederacy sent two diplomats, James Mason and John Slidell, to Great Britain and France to pursue diplomatic relations with the British. The ship they sailed on, the *RMS Trent* was intercepted by an American naval vessel and the two diplomats were seized by Union officials.

This action caused outrage in both Great Britain and the United States. The British argued that this was against the rules of war and they demanded the release of the diplomats and a formal apology by the United States. Americans, meanwhile, were outraged that the British were considering diplomatic relations with the Confederacy. Many Americans wanted to go to war with Great Britain. Indeed, war was a looming threat for several weeks until the release of Mason and Slidell ended the crisis.

The Naval War

At the outset of the war, the Union had a naval advantage over the Confederacy. This was for a couple of reasons. First, the majority of shipbuilding was done in the northern ports of New England. In fact, the only major port in the South was New Orleans. Second, the South was an agrarian society and the North had the industrial resources and power to produce a major navy while the South did not.

The first major naval battle was a big first not only in American history but also in world history. It occurred off Hampton Roads, Virginia, and it was the first battle between two ironclad warships. The *USS Monitor* and *CSS Virginia* (formerly the *USS Merrimack*) clashed and fought over the course of two days but the battle ended inconclusively.

The rest of the naval war was characterized by the Union blockade of Southern ports and the attempt by Confederate ships to run this blockade, seldom successfully.

The Union navy sent a naval fleet under command of David Farragut to take the port of New Orleans. Farragut succeeded after winning decisive victories at Fort Jackson and Fort St. Phillip in Louisiana.

The Confederacy's main forte in the naval war was privateering. Confederate ships ran the blockade and wreaked havoc on Northern commerce in the Atlantic and even the Pacific Ocean.

Eventually the blockade on the South accomplished what it set out to achieve and the Southern economy suffered significantly.

The Battle of Shiloh

The South had an ill-equipped army but it had superior generals. This was something that the North lacked for the most part. One exception was General Ulysses S. Grant. He was a West Point graduate and had proven to be a competent general. He led the Union to victory at Fort Henry and Fort Donelson, Tennessee in early 1862.

The Confederate army under the command of Albert Johnston and P.G.T Beauregard attacked the Union forces in Southwestern Tennessee at Shiloh. The first day of fighting was fierce and ended with moderate Confederate advantages but the Union forces regrouped during the second day of the battle. Johnston was killed in action and the Confederate assault was repulsed.

Rumors spread that Grant was drunk during the battle and his public image suffered. Many people wanted him to be removed from command but Lincoln replied "I can't spare this man, he fights."

The Union campaign in Tennessee continued and the Union army captured Memphis in June 1862. They bombarded Chattanooga soon afterwards.

The Seven Day Battle and Lee's Maryland Campaign

Battles continued to rage throughout Virginia. The Confederacy won the majority of these battles under the qualified leadership of Robert E. Lee. Union General George McClellan was advancing on Richmond when he and Lee clashed in several battles from June 25 to July 1, 1862. This series of engagements was called the Seven Day Battle. The largest of the battles was the Battle of Gaines Mill. It was fought on June 27 and ended in a Confederate victory. McClellan would eventually win the last battle of the seven at Malvern Hill but he retreated from the Richmond area. The majority of the Seven Day Battle was inconclusive and indecisive. Meanwhile, Lee attacked Union General John Pope and defeated him at the Second Battle of Manassas. Pope was forced to retreat and the Confederacy's campaign in Virginia continued to do quite well.

This encouraged Lee to invade the northern state of Maryland. He was defeated by McClellan at South Mountain and was engaged by him again at the bloody battle of Antietam. Antietam was one of the most important battles of the war. First, it ended Lee's Maryland campaign. Second, it dissuaded the governments of Britain and France from intervening as some suspected would happen sooner or later. Finally, it was the necessary victory that Abraham Lincoln needed to establish his Emancipation Proclamation, the freeing of all slaves. He hesitated to do this before Antietam because he did not want to lose the support of the border states: Kentucky, Maryland, Delaware and West Virginia, all of which supported slavery. Lincoln's fear was that these states would switch sides if he freed the slaves. After Antietam, he was confident however that the Union would remain strong and so he proclaimed all slaves free.

Antietam has been credited as being the turning point in the Civil War.

> *Thinking More About It* — The failure of Lee's attack at Antietam can be largely attributed to the Providence of God. McClellan's troops found Lee's battle plans wrapped in a cigar and brought it back to McClellan. McClellan therefore gained an advantage over the Confederates which eventually resulted in the end of Lee's Maryland campaign. Lee himself believed in God's providence. After the Civil War he wrote, "We failed but in the good Providence of God apparent failure often proves a blessing".

The Battle of Perryville

Another battle that, in ways very similar to the Battle of Antietam, was important in turning the course of the war in favor of the Union was the Battle of Perryville, fought at Perryville, Kentucky on October 8, 1862. Confederate general Braxton Bragg had invaded Kentucky in June and had clashed with Union forces under the main command of Don Carlos Buell throughout the summer and autumn. Bragg and his subordinate general Leonidas Polk clashed with Buell's Union army at Perryville and eventually forced the Union forces to retreat. Although this battle was technically a tactical victory for the Confederacy it was an important strategic victory for the Union. Bragg withdrew from Kentucky for good soon after the battle, thus ending the Kentucky campaign.

The Emancipation Proclamation

As of New Year's Day of 1863 President Abraham Lincoln declared the Emancipation Proclamation, freeing all the slaves. Lincoln was confident to take this step because of the recent victory the Union had won at Antietam as well as the end of Confederate Braxton Bragg's Kentucky Campaign. There was also a movement to arm slaves and freemen to fight in the war for the Union. Incidentally, there may have been inklings of abolition in the South during the war. Both African-American and white Confederate soldiers received the same pay. In the North, whites were paid more than blacks.

The Battles of Fredericksburg and Chancellorsville

McClellan's hesitance to attack Lee after Antietam led to his loss of command and he was replaced by General Ambrose Burnside. (Incidentally, Burnside popularized the hairstyle known as sideburns.) Burnside planned to surprise Lee by attacking him at Fredericksburg but he had to wait for the pontoon bridges to arrive so his troops could cross the Rappahannock River. The pontoon bridges were delayed however and any attempt to surprise Lee failed. Instead the Confederates repulsed the Union troops from Fredericksburg with heavy losses. After Fredericksburg, Burnside was replaced by Joseph Hooker. Hooker led the Union Army of the Potomac to attack Robert E. Lee's Army of Northern Virginia in April 1863. The two forces battled at Chancellorsville, Virginia over the course of a week. Lee took a risk, dividing his force in two, but this turned out to be a very successful strategy. Union General Joseph Hooker was confused and unsure of his own movements so the battle was a rout in favor of Lee and the Confederates. Chancellorsville was called "Lee's Perfect Battle". The only thing that stained this otherwise perfect Confederate victory was the death of Stonewall Jackson. Jackson and his officers were mistaken for Union cavalry by Confederate troops and Jackson was shot and died later of pneumonia. Lee likened the loss of Jackson to the loss of his own right arm.

Cool Fact

Stonewall Jackson was a strong, Presbyterian Christian. He was even nicknamed "Old Blue Lights" by his men. This nickname was due to his Christian zeal and fervor. He hated to fight on Sundays and many times avoided it. Jackson once said that "My religious belief teaches me to feel as safe in battle as I do in bed." Stonewall's nickname can certainly be applied to his faith. He was a religious stone wall. He was one of the greatest Confederate generals and also a great man of God.

The Vicksburg Campaign

While Lee was winning in Virginia, Grant was invading Mississippi. Grant defeated the Confederates at Port Gibson, Raymond and Jackson in the first few weeks of May, 1863. He then dealt the Confederacy heavy blows at Champion Hill and Big Black River Bridge. This enabled him to put the Confederate fortress of Vicksburg, Mississippi under siege. It was surrendered to him on Independence Day, 1863. Just days later the Siege of Port Hudson, Louisiana ended with its capture by Union troops, thus putting the final Confederate fortress on the Mississippi River in Union hands.

The Battle of Gettysburg

In June 1863, Lee won another victory over the Union at the Second Battle of Winchester. This enabled him to take the war to the Union by invading Pennsylvania. Union General George Meade was sent to drive Lee from Northern soil.

Confederate troops marched into Gettysburg to pick up shoes for the army and the largest battle in the history of North America began when they clashed with Union troops. The two armies met at Gettysburg and fought a three-day battle from July 1-3, 1863. Meade showed excellent strategic leadership skills during the battle. Finally after three days of fighting, Lee's army retreated and the bloodiest, largest battle of the American Civil War was over.

Meade and Lee's armies continued to fight smaller battles as Lee retreated through Maryland. They clashed at the inconclusive battles of Williamsport and Boonsboro days after Gettysburg.

In November 1863, Abraham Lincoln gave his famous "Gettysburg Address" at the battlefield, hallowing it and establishing a cemetery there.

THE BATTLE OF GETTYSBURG

The Battle of Chickamauga

The war in Tennessee was still progressing. In September 1863, William Rosencrans led his Union army across the Tennessee River and into Georgia. They met a Confederate force under Braxton Bragg at Chickamauga and suffered a defeat. Rosencrans was bottled up in Chattanooga, Tennessee.

Grant led reinforcements to Chattanooga and defeated the Confederates in several battles around Chattanooga. These included the assaults on Lookout Mountain and Missionary Ridge. Grant not only relieved Rosencrans' besieged force but also took Chattanooga, driving Bragg out of Tennessee and setting the stage for William T. Sherman to invade Georgia.

The Battle of the Wilderness

Grant moved north from Tennessee to Virginia. He and Lee clashed for the first time in Spotsylvania County, Virginia in May 1864. This first battle between the two great generals ended in an inconclusive "tie". This began a war of attrition between Grant and Lee in Virginia. The second major battle in this war of attrition was the Battle of Spotsylvania Court House, another inconclusive draw. The Confederates defeated the Union at Cold Harbor. The Union advanced towards Richmond, the capital of the Confederacy, but they were repelled at the Second Battle of Petersburg.

Meanwhile the Confederates under Jubal Early had invaded Maryland. They won at the battle of Monocacy and advanced to Washington, D.C. Early's army was repelled at the Battle of Fort Stevens in the District of Columbia itself. This battle was observed by Abraham Lincoln himself and he was shot at by the Confederate lines.

Early's forces were defeated soundly at Rutherford's Farm, Virginia a little over a week after their attack on the U.S. capital. Grant sent Phillip Sheridan's cavalry to chase Early back towards Richmond.

Sherman's March to the Sea

After the battle of Chattanooga, in which he had taken part, Union General William Tecumseh Sherman invaded Georgia, driving towards Atlanta. He was engaged in a series of battles by Confederate General Joseph Johnston around Atlanta. Sherman's troops won at Jonesborough in early

September 1864 and the city of Atlanta fell to him the day after the battle. After capturing Atlanta, Sherman marched through Georgia to the city of Savannah on the coast during his famous (and to Southerners, infamous) "march to the sea".   As he marched through Georgia, and later the Carolinas, he destroyed crops, telegraph lines and railroads in an attempt to destroy the South's economy and transportation system. Eventually Johnston surrendered to him in North Carolina.

The End of the War

In April 1865, Grant defeated Lee at the Third Battle of Petersburg in Virginia. A few days later at the Battle of Sayler's Creek, Grant won again. Eventually the two armies met for one final battle at Appomattox Court House, Virginia. It was there that Lee surrendered to Grant and the American Civil War was officially over. The Union forces cheered but Grant silenced them.

Cool Fact
Lee's official surrender occurred in a house occupied by Wilmer McLean and his family. Ironically, McLean had been acquainted with the war before. The First Battle of Manassas, one of the earliest battles of the war, had been fought around his home and a cannonball had even been shot into his kitchen. He moved his family to escape the war only to find that it would end in his very own parlor.

Past, Present, Future — One major, yet subtle, result of the Civil War was a change in the American mindset. Before the war, people said that the United States *were*, indicating a certain individuality and independence among the states. After the war, people began saying that the United States *was*. The focus was taken off the *States* and instead on the *United.* How do you view your relationship to your country and state today?

THE SURRENDER AT APPOMATTOX

Reconstruction

The war was over but the work of putting the country back together was just beginning. The U.S. government had to set about the task of piecing the nation back together. This process is called Reconstruction. It would be a long, hard process for sure. During the war Lincoln had created the Ten-Percent Plan. This plan was meant to readmit Southern states back into the Union if at least ten percent of the voting population voted to be readmitted. Only those that had voted for readmission could hold public office in that state.

Many Congressmen hated the idea. They wanted to punish the South for the war. They saw Lincoln's plan as too lenient.

Lincoln was assassinated on April 15, 1865, just about a week after the war ended. While watching a play at Ford's Theatre, Lincoln was shot by a radical pro-Soutehrn actor named John Wilkes Booth. At first the audience thought that the shots were part of the performance. Booth jumped onto the stage from the balcony where Lincoln had been seated, screaming "Sic Semper Tyrannis!", Latin for "Thus always to tyrants." The nation mourned the loss of Lincoln and his Vice-President Andrew Johnson became President. Despite the hopes that Congress had that Johnson would be more punitive in his reconstruction policies, they were disappointed. Johnson preferred more gentle measures. The Congress and Johnson fought throughout the rest of the term over Reconstruction policy. Eventually this political battle ended in Johnson's impeachment by the House of Representative. Ulysses S Grant, the Union war hero, was elected President in 1868.

Grant himself was a good, honest man but he was a soldier, not a politician. He was a naive President and relied on the advice of his close friends who were not always as good and honest as Grant was. A series of scandals plagued Grant's administration. Many of these scandals involved corrupt politicians in Grant's administration taking bribes from big businesses.

Meanwhile, the Congress imposed considerably harsh reconstruction terms on the South. The South was put under military occupation. They were also forced to recognize the rights of freedmen (freed slaves) and extend the suffrage (right to vote) to male freedmen. Despite the fact that they were free, the situations of a vast majority of freedmen did not improve. Many worked on the same plantations as they had when they were slaves, with a meager income. Laws were imposed on them to lower their standard of living and keep them from enjoying full civil rights. Radical whites banded together into groups like the Ku Klux Klan to terrorize freedmen and they lynched and killed many Black Southerners. It reminds me of the plight of the Israelites when they were advancing on the Jordan River in Exodus. They grumbled to Moses, saying that slavery was better than starving in the wilderness. Indeed, there was no major improvement from slavery to freedom in the early days of Reconstruction.

The Election of 1876

The presidential election of 1876 was one of the most controversial elections in American history. It also had a major part to play in ending Reconstruction. The Republican nominee was Rutherford B. Hayes of Ohio. The Democrat nominee was Samuel Tilden of New York. Tilden had an impressive resume. His big claim to fame was the part he played in breaking William "Boss" Tweed's Tammany Hall political machine, a corrupt ring of money-grabbing politicians in New York. The Republicans' main campaign strategy was to wave the "bloody shirt" by equating Democrats to Confederates.

Tilden won the most electoral votes, a total of 184. He was one vote short of winning the necessary majority. 20 electoral votes were disputed. In three Southern states there were suspicions of fraud and corruption. In Oregon, one elector's vote was disputed because of his supposed illegal appointment.

This led to the creation of a fifteen-man committee to decide the election once and for all. The committee was made up of ten congressmen and five supreme court justices. Seven Republicans and seven Democrats and one Independent were selected. The Independent party committee member however stepped down to take his seat in the Senate. This left only Republicans in the Supreme Court. Another was appointed to the committee, leaving the committee with eight Republicans and seven Democrats. Hayes won by a vote of 8-7 along straight party lines.

There was much controversy over the election and the South was upset because Tilden had carried much of the South. In order to appease the South, Hayes promised to end Reconstruction when he took office. Reconstruction did end, as Hayes promised, in 1877.

Chapter Seven

The Development of American Society

The Industrial Revolution

The latter half of the nineteenth century was characterized by the growth of industry in America. America became the world's leading producer of steel and other materials during this period. Several inventions changed American society and many of these were introduced during this period. Trains and railways had been introduced back in the early 1800s and they were used to a considerable degree during the Civil War. Railways crisscrossed the country and the first trans-continental railway (railroad crossing the entire continent) was completed in 1869. The last spike was driven in at Promontory, Utah Territory. Trains had proved revolutionary during the Civil War and both sides sent raiding parties to destroy enemy train tracks in an attempt to slow down the enemy. Railroads made many men rich. The legendary George Vanderbilt, who built America's largest home, the Biltmore Estate in North Carolina, gained a part of his vast wealth through the railroad business.

There was also considerable interest growing in pursuing flight. Hot air balloons had been used by Union reconnaissance scouts during the Civil War. In 1903, Wilbur and Orville Wright flew for the first time at Kitty Hawk, North Carolina. The invention of the airplane was also revolutionary and it too was soon used as a tool of reconnaissance during the First World War.

The Civil War had also been the first war in which two ironclad ships had fought together in the same battle. American naval commanders continued to design innovative naval ships. In 1907, the American naval "Great White Fleet" circumnavigated the globe in a show of American naval strength by order of President Theodore Roosevelt.

The telephone was also invented during this time. Alexander Graham Bell made the first telephone call to his assistant in 1876. Thomas Edison also experimented with sound technology, inventing the phonograph in 1878. Edison is also famous for inventing the Kinetoscope, the first motion picture camera, and of course, the electric light bulb.

These inventions revolutionized society and made the innovators of America very rich.

With the growth of industry came a number of men who made fortunes in their business ventures. These "captains of industry" included men like Andrew Carnegie and John D. Rockefeller. Carnegie was originally a poor

Scottish immigrant who worked his way up the ladder and eventually became the owner of Bessemer Steel Company. Rockefeller was the son of an often-absent shady salesmen. He too worked his way up the ladder and founded Standard Oil Company in 1870. Standard Oil became one of the most successful businesses in the country and soon created a monopoly on the oil industry. Rockefeller is sometimes said to be the richest man in history when inflation is taken into account. Both Carnegie and Rockefeller embodied an economic system called capitalism. Capitalism held that little government intervention in the economy was needed and that left to itself, the economy would grow significantly. Although quite a few innovators and businessmen grew rich the majority of Americans did not. Many of these poorer Americans worked for the captains of industry as factory workers. Even children worked for their families during this time. Working conditions were very bad and pay was low. Many workers wanted reform in the workplace so they grouped together into labor unions. Labor unions crusaded for better pay and working conditions for workers. Sometimes these attempts at reform got ugly. During an 1886 demonstration in Chicago's Haymarket Square a bomb exploded and police gunned down the protesters, killing four of them. Seven police officers were killed as well. The "Haymarket Riot," as it became to be known as was further aggravated when eight anarchists were convicted of conspiracy and several of them were hanged.

THE HAYMARKET RIOT

In 1894, workers at Pullman Railroad Company went on strike after receiving pay cuts. This strike was massive and literally shut down the country's railroad system west of Chicago for several days. President Grover Cleveland ordered federal troops out to end the strike, much to the protest of the Governor of Illinois. The troops cracked down on the strikers. Thirty people were killed and others wounded. This move by President Cleveland made him unpopular and ruined his chance for reelection in 1896.

Thinking More About It — Which would you side with, the corporations or unions? Why?

The Economic Policy of the American Federal Government

Many people wanted the government to break up monopolies like Rockefeller's Standard Oil. These monopolies were called trusts. They were business that had grown so much that they crowded out their competition and dominated their industry. In the case of Standard Oil, Rockefeller's business dominated the oil industry, stifling competition.

In 1890, Congress passed the Sherman Anti-Trust Act. This legislation was meant to break trusts and prevent them from becoming so dominant in their industry.

There was also great debate in the federal government over tariffs. Tariffs had been part of American political debate since the very early days. Tariffs were taxes on imports into the United States. These taxes were meant to discourage importing goods from other countries thereby encouraging production and economic integrity in the United States itself. Some Americans felt that tariffs led to the building of trusts and so they opposed them. President Cleveland opposed tariffs but President William McKinley supported them. Among other reasons, McKinley's support for tariffs may have contributed to his victory in the Presidential election of 1896 over Cleveland.

Another economic policy that became central to American political debate during the late 1800s and early 1900s was the debate over Free Silver.

The basis of the Free Silver debate was whether the United States should use silver as currency. The silver would be coined and used at a 16 to 1 ratio with gold. This meant that every once of gold would be worth sixteen ounces of silver. Free silver was feared to drive gold out of circulation. William Jennings Bryan was one of the leaders of the Free Silver movement and he ran on that platform during several Presidential elections, losing them all. Eventually the Free Silver movement lost momentum and the nation moved back to the Gold Standard.

Another contender in the debate over currency was the short-lived Greenback Party. This movement sought to use paper dollar bills as the basis of value in the economy. It became a powerful third party for some time but gradually faded away.

American Politics During the Industrial Revolution

American politics during the first few decades after the Civil War was dominated by an entity called the political machine. The political machines were essentially political organizations that promoted their own members for public office, often using corrupt means to influence elections.

The biggest political machine was a democratic one in New York City called the Tammany Hall machine. It was overseen by William "Boss" Tweed. Tweed grew quite rich on the corruption of the machine. One of the primary reasons for his downfall was Thomas Nast's political cartoons which mocked him. Samuel Tilden, who ran against Rutherford Hayes in the 1876 Presidential Election, also claimed to have "broken Boss Tweed". Tweed's ring of corruption ended in his second imprisonment by Samuel Tilden in the 1870s.

The Democratic Party was not the only group to experience scandals. There were political machines at work in the Republican Party as well. During President Ulysses Grant's administration from 1869-1877 the Republican-dominated government was hit hard with several scandals. The Black Friday Scandal involved two businessmen, Jim Fiske and Jay Gould, who manipulated the gold market for their own personal gain. The Credit Mobilier Scandal involved the bribing of members of Congress to overlook the illegal dealings of the Union Pacific Railroad Company. The Whiskey Ring Scandal involved illegal dealings among government officials concerning the whiskey tax. All in all, these scandals did affect Grant's public image but he was reelected in 1872 nonetheless. This was mainly because of the weakness of his opponent, Horace Greeley.

The Pendleton Civil Service Reform Act

In 1880, James Garfield, yet another Republican, replaced Hayes as President. However, shortly into his administration he was shot in a train station by Charles Guiteau. The mentally ill Guiteau had been seeking a job in the government ever since Garfield's election. He thought he deserved one because of what he saw as his great contribution to Garfield's victory. Guiteau was later executed. Immediately before his execution, he showed his mental instability by dancing up to the place of execution and reciting poetry.

Garfield was succeeded by his Vice-President Chester Arthur. Arthur surprised many people with his honesty. One of the many reforms that Arthur passed during his presidency was the Pendleton Civil Service Reform Act, which based political appointment on personal merit rather than money or status.

Immigration During the Industrial Revolution

Throughout the nineteenth century, immigrants had been steadily flowing into the United States. At first, many of these were from Ireland, Great Britain and Germany but as the century progressed immigrants arrived from all around the world. Many Jews, Russians, Italians and Chinese also immigrated to America especially during the latter half of the century. Many of these immigrants arrived in New York City and were processed into the country at the legendary Ellis Island. The Statue of Liberty was erected in 1886 and soon became an icon of freedom and opportunity all around the world. New York City itself was divided into neighborhoods where certain ethnic groups lived. Many Chinese lived in "Chinatown". Italians settled in "Little Italy". "Hell's Kitchen" was a predominately Irish neighborhood.

Eventually, the national attitude towards immigration grew increasingly hostile. Immigrants, it was said, took jobs away from native citizens. The Chinese were an especially discriminated-against ethnic minority. There was even legislation passed to bar Chinese from entering the United States. The Chinese Exclusion Act was passed in 1882 and closed the doors of America to Chinese for ten years.

Political Parties

With the arrival of immigrants came the arrival of new ideas and philosophies. With the strong influx of Germans came "radical" ideas such as socialism and anarchism. Socialism was incredibly strengthened with the writings of Karl Marx in the mid-1800s. Socialism was built on the idea that inequality between social classes was evil and must be destroyed. Marx saw the primary problem with society as the warfare between these classes. The goal of Socialism was to destroy the divisions between social classes so that everyone was equal. Socialism appealed to many Americans because of the large working class. The Socialist Party of America was formed in 1901. Eugene V. Debs ran for President on the Socialist ticket, gaining more than 900,000 votes on more than one occasion. Before that, the Workingmen's Party, which embraced Marxist doctrine, was the forerunner of the Socialist party. It was founded in 1876. The main goal of the Workingmen's Party was to crusade for labor reform. Several other smaller labor parties also emerged during this time. In 1906, Upton Sinclair wrote the novel "The Jungle" which exposed working conditions in the meat-packing industry. This novel did much to bring about social change in the industrial cities.

Anarchism, far more radical than Socialism, was a political ideology that spurned all authority. Anarchy comes from the Greek words *ana* and *arkhos* which together mean "no ruler". Anarchy is a philosophy that calls for no government at all. Anarchists were also active in America. The eight men convicted of the Haymarket bombing were also anarchists. President William McKinley was assassinated by an anarchist at the Pan-American Exposition in Buffalo,

New York in 1901. The three prominent anarchists in late nineteenth century America were Johann Most, Emma Goldman and Alexander Berkmann. Most theorized the "Propaganda of the Deed" theory. This idea called for violent actions against the "enemies of the people". As a result many Anarchists resorted to terrorist bombings and attacks. Johann Most even wrote and distributed literature demonstrating how to build bombs. Goldman was a radical feminist who was inspired to embrace anarchy after the Haymarket Riot. Berkmann was a native Russian and a good friend and close associate of Goldman.

Despite the rise of socialism and anarchism, the two main political forces in the United States remained: the Republican Party and the Democratic Party. The Democratic party could trace its origins back to Thomas Jefferson's Democratic-Republican Party. (Yes, at one time there was a party called the Democratic-Republican Party. I know, it's ironic.) This later evolved into Andrew Jackson's Democratic Party. The Democrats were split by the issue of slavery. The radical, pro-slavery, Southern Democratic Party emerged on the eve of the Civil War. The Democrats dominated the South during Reconstruction and afterwards.

The Republican Party had grown out of Alexander Hamilton's Federalist Party. The Federalists lost their power after the War of 1812 and were replaced by the anti-Jacksonian Whigs. The Whigs faded away as well and during the 1850s linked up with radical abolitionists and the anti-foreigner Know-Nothing Party to form what would be known as the Republican Party. The Republicans progressed significantly under Abraham Lincoln and dominated the presidency during Reconstruction. Grover Cleveland was the only Democrat, post-Civil War, president until Woodrow Wilson's election in 1912.

The Greenback and People's Parties also took the stage for a time during the late 1800s, but eventually faded away. The Greenbacks were built on the policy of paper money and increased inflation. The People's Party, (also called the Populist Party), was popular with Midwestern farmers. It was built on the policy of freely coined silver (the Free Silver movement).

African Americans also established their own political presence. The greatest African-American political and social thinker of the time was W.E.B. Dubois. He established the National Association for the Advancement of Colored People which campaigned for civil rights for African-Americans. Marcus Garvey led the "Back to Africa" movement in the early 1900s.

Meanwhile, African-Americans were taking great steps towards political active involvement. The first African-American to serve in the US Congress was Hiram Revels of Mississippi, who served from 1870-1871. He opened the way for other African-Americans to serve in the American government.

CHAPTER EIGHT

AMERICAN TERRITORIAL EXPANSION

Westward Expansion and Indian Wars

The United States continued its westward expansion during and after the Civil War. As Americans moved west they came into contact with Native Americans. Many times these meetings were hostile. After the Civil War, the main influx of American settlers settled in the Great Plains. The Native American nations that populated the Great Plains included the Sioux, Apache and others.

The Federal government's policy towards Native Americans was centered around moving them to approved areas of protected land called reservations. The U.S. army was used to forcibly remove the Native Americans to these reservations. Many Native Americans resisted. This resulted in a series of bloody wars between the U.S. army and the Native Americans which eventually ended in 1890 at the Wounded Knee Massacre.

Great Plains Conflicts

During the Civil War, Sioux warriors in Minnesota fought the US army in the 1862 Dakota War. This war eventually ended in Sioux defeat and the execution of Sioux leaders in Mankato, Minnesota. In 1865 war broke out in Colorado between the Cheyenne and Arapaho nations and American settlers. The US army massacred Native Americans at Sand Creek. In retaliation, the Native Americans massacred American settlers before moving into Nebraska.

Two Union generals who had fought in the Civil War, Phillip Sheridan and George Custer, were the two main generals who campaigned against the Native Americans in the West.

Sheridan was in control of the entire American campaign in the West and was a sworn enemy of Native Americans. Custer destroyed a Native American camp and massacred its inhabitants at the Battle of Washita River in 1868.

When a gold rush began in the Dakota Territory in the 1870s, the Sioux once again went on the warpath. During the Sioux War of 1876-1877 Custer made his infamous blunder. He and a small, outnumbered force of US cavalry were attacked by Lakota Native Americans and their allies near the Little Bighorn River in the Montana Territory. Custer and his entire force were slaughtered. The Lakota were led by Crazy Horse. A Sioux chieftain named Sitting Bull had a vision of a great Native American victory. This inspired the Lakota to their triumph at Little Bighorn.

CUSTER AT LITTLE BIGHORN

The End of Hostilities

The end of major Native American hostilities came in 1890 when US troops massacred Lakota at Wounded Knee, South Dakota. They were provoked by the Lakota's Ghost Dance and felt threatened. There remained a few, scattered, minimal conflicts across the West until 1924. Mormon settlers clashed with Native Americans in Utah during 1914-1915 and again in 1923. In 1924, the Apache War ended, thus officially ending the Native American Wars.

Thinking More About It — Do you think it was right for the United States to confiscate Native American territory?

Continued Territorial Expansion

The United States continued to acquire territorial possessions, both on the North American continent and elsewhere. The first of these was the acquisition of Alaska in 1867.

That year, William Seward, the Secretary of State, secured the territory of Alaska through a treaty with Russia. Russia sold Alaska to the United States mainly because they feared that they would lose to Great Britain in a war.

Many people thought that Seward was foolish for purchasing Alaska and so the deal became known as "Seward's Folly".

The biggest precursor to the annexation of Hawaii was missionary activity. The Americans sent missionaries to Hawaii during the late 1800s. Eventually, some Americans wanted to annex Hawaii (add it to their territory). Grover Cleveland refused but his successor William McKinley did not. Hawaii was annexed in 1898 and officially became a territory in 1900.

The Spanish-American War

There was considerable debate among Americans in the late 1800s over the issue of colonies and territorial possessions overseas. Imperialists wanted America to join in the colonizing spree that the European powers had gone on. They wanted the United States to expand its territory into the Pacific and Latin America. Anti-Imperialists thought that this notion was hypocritical because the United States had been the former colonies of another country. They stated that to establish American colonies would be against the wishes of our founding fathers. One prominent Imperialist was William McKinley. Mark Twain was a prominent voice in the Anti-Imperialist movement.

Meanwhile, Spain, once the greatest power on the American continents, was fighting rebels in Cuba. Americans supported the Cuban rebels and lurid, often exaggerated, stories of Spanish brutality were circulated throughout the United States. Many Americans wanted the United States to go to war with Spain in support of Cuba.

In 1898, the American battleship, USS Maine entered Havana harbor in Cuba to protect US interests. It mysteriously blew up on the night of February 15, 1898. Although the causes of the explosion remain unknown it was suspected that the Spanish had blown the ship up on purpose. This view was circulated through the United States and by April the two countries were at war.

THE USS MARINE

The Caribbean Campaign

Immediately after war was declared on April 25, the US Navy bombard Matanzas, Cuba and American troops landed in Cuba at Guantanamo Bay in early June. Later in that same month they landed at Daiquiri only to find the area deserted. The Spanish repulsed another landing at Tayacoba, Cuba on June 30. The Americans advanced to Santiago. It was during the battles around Santiago that one of the most famous charges in American history occurred. Theodore Roosevelt and his "Rough Riders" charged up San Juan Hill and routed a Spanish force on the top of the hill. Santiago was besieged and taken in mid-July.

The United States army also invaded Puerto Rico. They took Mayaguez in early August. By then the Spanish had had enough and surrendered.

> *Cool Fact*
>
> More men died of tropical diseases during the Spanish-American War than died in battle.

The Pacific Campaign

The majority of the war was fought in Cuba but a good deal of fighting also occurred in the Spanish territory of the Philippines. The US Asiatic Squadron under George Dewey sailed into Manila Bay when war first broke out. The Spanish engaged them at the battle of Manila Bay on May 1. The battle was one of the most one-sided victories in history. Dewey's fleet destroyed the entire Spanish Pacific Squadron without losing a single ship. In fact, he lost only one seaman to heat stroke in the entire battle. Dewey's words to his subordinate commander soon became famous: "You may fire when ready Gridley". A series of smaller engagements occurred on the mainland, ending in the American capture of Manila itself. The United States also seized the Pacific Islands of Guam and Wake Island in June.

The Results of the Spanish-American War

Almost as soon as it had begun the Spanish-American War was over. Some Americans called it the "splendid little war". Cuba became independent as a result of the war. Puerto Rico, Guam and Wake Island went to the United

States. So did the Philippines, for a price of twenty million dollars.

The Philippines continued fighting against American rule just as they had done against the Spanish. This led to the Philippine-American War which lasted several years. It was later called "America's first Vietnam" because of the guerrilla tactics of Emilio Aguinaldo and his Filipino troops. Eventually Aguinaldo was captured and his men defeated in 1902.

Thinking More About It — Do you think that the Spanish American War was justified? Why or why not?

American Foreign Policy in Asia

During the turn of the twentieth century, the United States expanded its horizons beyond North America and became minimally involved in world affairs. Around 1900 Secretary of State John Hay established his Open Door policy with China. This policy called for free trade between the United States and China as well as a declaration, made to European nations, of American trade rights with China. During this period in history, China was in danger of being carved into pieces by the more powerful countries surrounding it. Japan, Russia, France, Britain and Germany all made claims to Chinese trade and Chinese territory. Hay's Open Door policy attempted to alleviate the tension of growing territorial disputes by suggesting that the Great

Powers "share" access to Chinese trade and markets. American troops also intervened in Chinese affairs in 1899 when the Qing dynasty was threatened by anti-foreigner rebels. These rebels, who called themselves the Society of Righteous Harmonious Fists, rose up against foreign influence in China in the fall of 1899. The Europeans called these revolutionaries by the much more widely recognized name: the Boxers. The Boxer Rebellion ended in 1901 when troops from Europe, Japan and the United States invaded China and propped up the Qing government. The main American force to participate in the suppression of the Boxer Rebellion was the China Relief Expedition, an American force that, with the assistance of Europeans and Japanese, effectively ended the rebellion in the capital city of Peking (Beijing). During the battle in Peking, American troops scaled the Tartar Wall in the city and this soon became an iconic image of the Boxer Rebellion.

Later, President Theodore Roosevelt brought peace to Asia in 1905. He almost singlehandedly brought an end to the Russo-Japanese War at the Treaty of Portsmouth, New Hampshire.

The Panama Canal

The Monroe Doctrine, made in 1821, officially banned European powers from colonizing or intervening in the domestic affairs of North or South American countries. In 1904, President Theodore Roosevelt established the Roosevelt Corollary to the Monroe Doctrine. This gave the United States increased power to play "police" in the Western Hemisphere. The United States began to increasingly intervene in Central and South American affairs. One of the big reasons for the establishment of the Roosevelt Corollary, besides Roosevelt's personal imperialistic principles, was the Venezuelan Affair of 1902. This incident occurred between European countries and the South American nation of Venezuela. Germany and Britain began a naval blockade of Venezuela in 1902 because of debts that Venezuela had failed to pay. Roosevelt maintained US troops in Cuba to enforce the Monroe Doctrine and eventually the British and Germans withdrew.

One of the biggest interventions that Roosevelt undertook in Central America was the Panama Canal.

The idea of the Panama Canal was to build a canal through Panama so that ships didn't have to sail all the way around the tip of South America to get from the Pacific Ocean to the Atlantic Ocean. The French failed in this attempt during the 1880s and the torch soon passed on to the United States in the early 1900s. The Americans made a deal with Colombia, the country that owned Panama at the time, to build the canal but the Colombian government refused to recognize the treaty. So, Roosevelt told the Panamanians that if they declared independence from Colombia he would support them in their fight for freedom. True to his word, Roosevelt sent a fleet of US gunboats to Panama when the Panamanians declared independence. By 1903, Panama was independent and the United States had bought the rights to build a canal for ten million dollars. Construction on the canal began almost immediately. It was completed in 1914.

Cool Fact

Roosevelt is known for his famous saying, "Always speak softly and carry a big stick." Later, his policies in Central America became known as "Big Stick Diplomacy".

The Banana Wars

The Panama Canal was not the only operation undertaken by the Americans under the Roosevelt Corollary. A series of military interventions called the Banana Wars also occurred. Cuba was placed under US military occupation several times between 1898 and 1922. Nicaragua was under almost constant occupation between 1912 and 1933. US troops also landed in Honduras several times between 1903 and 1925. Haiti was invaded and occupied from 1915-1934. The Dominican Republic was also invaded in 1903 and again occupied from 1916-1924.

The Mexican Revolution

The largest military intervention that the US undertook in Central America was in Mexico. In 1910, a revolution against Mexican president Porfirio Diaz broke out and much fighting took place along the US-Mexico border. In fact, one of the rebel leaders, Francisco Madero, made his plans while gathering followers in Texas. In 1911 the town of Douglas,

Arizona was caught in the fighting and US troops increased along the border. After a confrontation between US sailors and Mexican troops at Tampico in 1914, President Woodrow Wilson asked Congress for permission to invade Mexico. Congress granted his request and the Mexican port of Veracruz was promptly occupied.

In 1916, Mexican rebel leader, Pancho Villa, led a raid on Columbus, New Mexico to seize supplies. He was repulsed by US troops. This incident led Wilson to send John Pershing into Mexico to track Villa down and kill him.

The Americans won the battle of Parral but lost at Carrizal. Eventually in 1917, US troops withdrew from Mexico, ending Pershing's Expedition.

The final major battle in the border war between the United States and Mexico was the battle of Ambos Nogales in 1918. Hostilities ceased entirely in 1919.

Although the border war between the United States and Mexico didn't have many major effects along the border itself, it did play an immense part in America's entrance into the First World War.

CHAPTER NINE

AMERICA ON THE WORLD STAGE

America's Involvement in the First World War

The First World War had begun in 1914 and at first, America had done a good job staying out of it. Although it did supply the Allied nations of Britain and France with arms and equipment, it nominally stayed neutral. Eventually, the Allies' enemy, Germany, began to use submarines to sink American shipping across the Atlantic. This was called unrestricted submarine warfare. The Germans justified this by condemning America's supplying of the Allies. In 1915, the most infamous of the submarine attacks occurred when the British ship *RMS Lusitania* was sunk. Onboard were more than one hundred Americans. Public outrage was stirred against Germany after the sinking of the *Lusitania*.

The US government attempted to make a deal with the Germans to stop unrestricted submarine warfare but the attacks continued.

Furthermore, tensions increased between the United States and Germany because of the revolutionary war in Mexico, which, on occasion, bled into the United States.

In 1917, British intelligence officers intercepted the Zimmermann Telegram, a telegram from the Germans to the Mexican government. In the telegram, the Germans promised to restore the states of Texas, Arizona and New Mexico to Mexico if Mexico agreed to join Germany's side in the war. The British agents sent the telegram on the United States, hoping to stir up popular opinion against Germany. It worked. In April 1917, Woodrow Wilson declared war on Germany.

The American Expeditionary Force (AEF) was organized and sent over to France. John Pershing, the American commander, announced as the Americans arrived in France, "Lafayette, we have arrived." The first major battle in which American troops participated was the Battle of Cantigny in 1918. They then participated in the battles of Belleau Wood and Chateau-Thierry. The US marines' most famous engagement of the war was Belleau Wood where they made an aggressive frontal assault on entrenched German forces, eventually causing them to flee. In honor of the Americans' sacrifice the French renamed the forest, the "Wood of the Marine Brigade".

Overall, the main effect of American entry into the war was a much-needed boost in morale among the British and French ranks. The Americans had not been in combat for too terribly long before the war ended in an Allied victory.

Wilson wanted to bring a painless peace to Europe. He drafted his "fourteen points" for world peace. The majority of the world rejected them. Wilson wanted to form an alliance to promote world peace, he called this idea the League of Nations. Unlike the failure of his Fourteen Points, the League of Nations succeeded considerably. Unfortunately for Wilson, many Americans, including some in Congress, didn't want the United States to join the League of Nations. The League of Nations was established in 1920 but the US Congress voted to stay out of it. After the Second World War, the League of Nations was replaced by the United Nations.

AMERICANS CHARGE DURING WORLD WAR I

Cool Fact

Machine guns and other modern weapons killed many men during the First World War but another enemy would destroy lives: both military and civilian without mercy or regard to nationality. This enemy supposedly originated from Spain. It was the infamous "Spanish Flu" or influenza. This virus killed millions of people worldwide.

American Society After the First World War

The First World War dramatically changed American society. Because of the need for men to fight, women had taken over production and many had gotten jobs at factories. The rise of women in the workforce brought about changes in women's society. There were also changes in the labor movement due to the Russian Revolution and the United States enjoyed a decade of prosperity called the "Roaring Twenties".

Women's Suffrage

The Women's Suffrage movement, the organized movement for women to gain the right to vote, can be traced back to the 1848 Seneca Falls Convention. This convention was organized by Lucretia Mott and Elizabeth Cady Stanton and became the foundation for the rest of the Women's Suffrage movement.

During the rise of industry in America, women continued to campaign for rights. Women's rights usually went hand-in-hand with other reform movements. Women were leading reformers in the Abolitionist movement and later the Temperance and Labor movements. Later crusaders for women's rights included Jane Addams, Julia Ward Howe and Susan B. Anthony.

In 1919, women were granted the right to vote. Their voice on Temperance was soon heard as intoxicating liquors became illegal before their official suffrage. Prohibition was a major result of the growing women's movement.

A WOMEN'S RIGHTS PARADE

The First Red Scare

Russia had experienced a Communist revolution in 1917 and the years after the First World War were filled with paranoia about radical political movements. This became known as the First Red Scare. (The Second Red Scare occurred in the 1950s after the Second World War. Reds were the name given to Bolshevik communists.) American troops had participated in an attempt to restore capitalism in Russia following the First World War. They militarily intervened by invading Siberia in what became known as the Polar Bear Expedition. Despite military action by the Allies, including the United States, the Bolsheviks retained control of Russia. Many Americans feared the rise of Bolshevism in America. Labor unions were increasing in strength and were increasingly growing radical. Anarchist and Communist groups were emerging within the labor unions and some Americans feared the worst--a Bolshevik revolution in the United States. In 1919, Seattle workers went on a general strike that lasted a week and practically shut down the city. Anarchist conspirators sent a series of bombs in the mail to prominent politicians and businessmen. The bomb plot failed but another series of bombings followed. These included the bombing of Attorney General Mitchell Palmer's house. Palmer began a "witch hunt" of radicals and began to deport them without trial. On May Day, 1919, riots occurred in Boston and Cleveland. Fighting occurred between radicals and more conservative Americans. Communist literature was burned by anti-radicals. Anarchists including Emma Goldman were deported.

Palmer predicted a major Red insurrection on May Day, 1920. The day passed with no such rebellion occurring. After this the fear of radicalism and communism died down.

The Race Riots of 1919

Communists were not the only group under attack during the year of 1919. African-Americans suffered as whites targeted them in a series of race riots during the "Red Summer" of 1919. The main reason for these race riots was the Great Migration of African-Americans from the rural South to the cities of the Midwest. As African-Americans arrived in the big cities, whites and blacks began to compete for jobs. This competition fueled the fires of the race riots. The riots were especially bad in Chicago, Washington D.C., Elaine, Arkansas and Omaha, Nebraska.

Hundreds died in the race riots and tensions between blacks and whites remained high.

Sacco and Vanzetti

Racism and prejudice were not aimed just at African-Americans however. In 1921, two Italian-born anarchists, Bartolomeo Vanzetti and Nicola Sacco, were accused of armed robbery and were tried. After a controversial trial they were found guilty and executed in 1927. This led to considerable public outrage and the trial and execution remained a controversy. Many accused the judges of prejudice against Sacco and Vanzetti's political opinions and of anti-Italian racism.

The Scopes Trial

Another major event occurred in 1925 that was arguably one of the most detrimental events to the Christian faith. The Scopes Trial was a legal case between John Scopes, a teacher, and the State of Tennessee. Scopes was on trial for violating Tennessee's law forbidding the theory of human evolution being taught in schools. William Jennings Bryan was chosen as the prosecuting attorney and the defense attorney was Clarence Darrow. The case soon became a philosophical showdown between modernism and Christian fundamentalism. In the end, Scopes was convicted but in the process Darrow made quick work of Bryan's intellectual reputation thus opening the door for future skepticism and eventually distrust in the Bible.

The Roaring Twenties

American society underwent major changes in the 1920s. This decade was commonly referred to as the roaring twenties. The feminist movement took off with the flapper movement, revolutionizing women's fashion. The mass production of the Model T car was made possible by Henry Ford's invention of the assembly line. This was also the Age of Jazz. Jazz greats like Louis Armstrong, Duke Ellington and George Gershwin delighted people with their music.

Sports also became popular during this period. Football, baseball and boxing dominated the sports scene during the roaring twenties.

A "Lost Generation" of American writers migrated to Europe during the period and revolutionized American literature. These included F. Scott Fitzgerald who wrote *The Great Gatsby*, a story about a mysterious high-class aristocrat in 1920s America and Ernest Hemingway, who is famous for many works, including *The Sun Also Rises, For Whom The Bell Tolls* and *The Old Man and the Sea*.

Prohibition made selling and consuming alcohol illegal. This did not stop criminals however. They continued to traffic illegal alcohol called "bathtub gin" into illegal bars called "speakeasies". This led to gang violence and organized crime in big cities like Chicago. Gangs and crime syndicates fought wars over the ownership of speakeasies.

The most famous crime boss of the time was Al Capone. His men struck against rival gangsters on Valentine's Day, 1929. The St. Valentine's Day Massacre was the killing of seven of Bugs Moran's gangsters in a warehouse in Chicago's North Side. Although most people thought that Capone was behind the killings, it was never fully investigated. Eventually Capone was arrested for tax evasion in 1931.

Meanwhile, on a more positive note, African-American urban culture flourished during the Harlem Renaissance. African-American poets such as Langston Hughes, philosophers such as Alain Locke and musicians such as Louis Armstrong were part of the movement, which was a revival of African-American culture in northern cities including New York City. The renaissance was named after the African-American neighborhood of Harlem in New York City.

The Great Depression

The prosperity of the roaring twenties ended when the stock market crashed in 1929. There were numerous reasons for this. For one, the growth in the 1920s economy had mainly benefited the rich and some, in the lower classes, stopped buying goods. As you can imagine this was detrimental to the economic market. Also, the Federal Reserve's monetary policy encouraged exaggerated speculation and many stock market transactions were in borrowed money. Although there are many theories as to why the Great Depression started, it can be probably blamed on unsound economic structure.

Herbert Hoover was the president of the United States when the Great Depression began. He attempted to stop the downfall of the economy but his policies failed. In the election of 1932, Hoover was easily defeated by Franklin D. Roosevelt.

The New Deal

Roosevelt soon put his "New Deal" into practice, stimulating the economy and reforming agricultural markets. He established the Public Works Administration which stimulated the economy through public construction projects such as roads and bridges. He also formed the Civilian Conservation Corps (CCC) to employ workers in government jobs such as the establishment of national parks. Roosevelt passed the Social Security Act in 1935, which gave pensions to the elderly. He also issued Executive Order 8802 to create the Fair Employment Practices Committee to crack down on job discrimination against African-Americans.

Slowly but surely, the economy managed to get itself back together but not until after Roosevelt's massive government intervention programs.

America Enters the Second World War

While Americans focused on fixing their broken economy, they tried their best to ignore what was going on in the rest of the world. Since 1933, the nation of Germany had been expanding its military and exercising considerable political power under the leadership of the Nazi party and Adolf Hitler. Italy, under Fascist leader Benito Mussolini was also seeking to expand. In Asia, the Japanese were moving into China and Japanese troops marched deeper and deeper into the Asian mainland.

In 1939, German troops invaded Poland leading Great Britain and France to declare war on the Third Reich (Nazi Germany). This set the Second World War in motion. Attempting to keep the United States out of the war, Roosevelt declared America neutral. However, the United States did agree to the Lend-Lease treaty with Great Britain in 1940. According to Lend-Lease, the United States would supply weapons and supplies to Great Britain in return for use of British military bases in North America and the West Indies. The German navy began to sink American shipping like it had during the First World War, to keep the supplies from reaching Great Britain. Roosevelt maintained American neutrality until December of 1941. On December 7, 1941, Japanese aircraft made a surprise attack on the US naval base in Pearl Harbor, Hawaii. Roosevelt called the attack on Pearl Harbor, "a day which will live in infamy". The United States promptly declared war on Japan and subsequently found itself at war with Germany and Italy as well.

The War in Europe

By the time the United States entered the Second World War, Germany had overrun France, the Low Countries, Scandinavia and the Balkans and were thrusting deeper and deeper into the Soviet Union (Russia). The only remaining Allied power in Western Europe was Great Britain. The British had managed to thwart an attempted invasion on their own country by driving the German air force from the British skies during the Battle of Britain in 1940. Meanwhile, British troops had clashed with Italian and German forces in North Africa, desperately defending Egypt. When America entered the war, US troops were shipped over to Great Britain and North Africa.

The first American offensive was Operation Torch, an invasion of key points along the North African coast in Algeria and Morocco. The Americans were mauled by the German army at the Battle of Kasserine Pass, Tunisia in 1943. Eventually the British and Americans achieved victory over the Germans and effectively conquered all of North Africa.

In July 1943, the Allies invaded Sicily, Italy and quickly conquered the island. Then they advanced on to the Italian mainland. By September, the Italian government had surrendered but German troops continued to defend the Italian peninsula against the Allies. The Allies made slow progress but eventually took Rome in June 1944.

D-Day

The biggest Allied invasion of the war occurred in June 1944 when Allied troops, mainly British, Americans and Canadians, landed in Normandy, France. This invasion was named Operation Overlord and the attack day was nicknamed D-Day. The Germans defended the beaches but were pushed back. Slowly but surely, Allied troops conquered Normandy. Then in late July, the Americans under General George Patton burst out of Normandy, broke through the German lines and overran France in a few short weeks. This was called the American Blitzkrieg. The Americans recaptured Paris in August. The British then invaded the Netherlands while the Americans pushed into Belgium. The British launched Operation Market Garden but they lost at the Battle of Arnhem. The conquest of the Netherlands would be painstakingly slow.

Meanwhile, the Americans were making slow headway in Belgium. They captured Aachen but failed to defeat the Germans at the Battle of the Hurtgen Forest. In the winter, the Germans counterattacked, invading the Ardennes Forest in Belgium. This caused a "bulge" to form in the American line, thus earning the battle its name: the Battle of the Bulge. During the Battle of the Bulge, American troops found themselves besieged in the town of Bastogne. After a long, hard siege, they were relieved by Patton's forces on Christmas Day, 1944.

In March 1945, the Americans captured the Remagen Bridge over the Rhine River and overran Western Germany. Meanwhile the Soviets were advancing from the east. The Soviets overran Austria, Poland, Hungary and Eastern

Germany. There was a brief "race to Berlin" between the Soviets and the Americans. This foreshadowed the future tensions and conflicts the two countries would experience. American troops met with Soviet forces at the Elbe River, thus effectively ending the war in Europe.

Sadly, one of the things that the Allied armies discovered as they advanced into Germany was the nasty legacy of German ideology and anti-Semitism. In a period of genocide called the Holocaust the Nazis exterminated millions of Jewish men, women and children, among others that they considered "unfit" for life. The Nazis' ideology was based on Herbert Spencer's theory of Social Darwinism: the idea that some members of society are more fit to live than others. This applied Darwin's idea of natural selection to not only biology, but human society as well. This "survival of the fittest" ideology was enforced by the Nazis' belief that the Pan-Germanic race, (the "Aryans") were morally, biologically and mentally superior to all other peoples. This was enforced by the existentialist philosophy of Frederick Nietzsche and his idea of "ubermensch" or "superman".

THE BATTLE OF THE BULGE

The War in the Pacific

After the attack on Pearl Harbor, the Japanese moved rapidly across the Pacific. They took Singapore from the British and took the Philippines from the United States. The Americans were finally able to stall Japanese forces moving towards Australia at the Battle of the Coral Sea. The major turning point in the Pacific war was the Battle of Midway in 1942. This was a decisive American naval victory that changed the course of the war in favor of the Allies.

From there the United States invaded the Solomon Islands and New Guinea in the South Pacific. They began a strategy of "island-hopping", slowly moving, island-by-island, through the Pacific towards Japan. The British,

Americans and Chinese fought Japanese armies in Burma in 1944, eventually driving them back from their primary goal: India. The failure of the Japanese attack on India was one of the biggest defeats they suffered in the war.

Also, by 1944, the Americans had advanced to the Philippines and recaptured them after much fighting. The most important naval battle in the Philippines Campaign was the Battle of Leyte Gulf.

THE FLAG IS RAISED AT IWO JIMA

Cool Fact

Paul tells young people, in 1 Timothy 4:12, to not let others discourage them because of their youth. One young lad of twelve years took that verse to heart when he enlisted in the US Navy and served aboard the USS South Dakota in the Pacific during the Second World War. He gained several medals including the prestigious Purple Heart but all his medals were taken from him when his age was found out. Decades later he appealed to Congress to receive them back and he did, with the exception of the Purple Heart. Many other young people fought in World War II. The Hitler Youth was a group of young, teenage German soldiers. Many Soviet teens and children fought for their motherland as well.

The End of the War

Americans attacked the islands of Iwo Jima and Okinawa in early 1945 and fought hard for these small islands. The Japanese would rather fight to the death than surrender and it soon became clear that if the United States invaded Japan itself, it would end in massive casualties for both sides. Meanwhile, the Soviet Union had declared war on Japan and invaded Manchuria, China and the island of Sakhalin off the coast of the Soviet Union.

In an attempt to win the war as quickly as possible, President Harry Truman, who had succeeded Roosevelt after his death in mid-1945, authorized the use of two atomic bombs, which had been secretly developed by the US Manhattan Project. In August 1945, the United States dropped these atomic bombs on the Japanese cities of Hiroshima and Nagasaki. The cities were practically flattened. The Japanese surrendered soon afterward.

The Potsdam Conference

The leaders of Great Britain, the Soviet Union and the United States met in Potsdam, Germany after the war ended to lay out plans for a post-war Europe. It was during this conference that the aims of the United States and the Soviet Union came to a full-fledged debate. Eventually, the conference ended with a mass of territory under direct or indirect Soviet control in Eastern Europe, including Eastern Germany, called the Eastern Bloc. Western Germany was divided into British, American and French zones and the capital city of Berlin, located in East Germany was also divided into US, British, French and Soviet zones.

The United States and the Soviet Union emerged from the war as the two most powerful countries in the world and this began a long period of rivalry and minimal conflict between the two superpowers. Because this never became a full-fledged war it is called the "Cold War", meaning that things had not heated up yet but relations were still cold between the two countries.

Visit www.highpointhistoryseries.com/bonuses/ for FREE bonus videos.

Conclusion

America had come a long way from the War for Independence, but that can be expected. History is dynamic and it is practically impossible to go any considerable amount of time without major changes occurring. The American Revolution put the nation on its feet. The Civil War kept the nation together and readied it for its soon-coming role on the world stage. From an isolated group of former colonies to one of the most powerful countries in the world, that was the trek that the United States had taken. But so much more was yet to be.

God's hand can be clearly seen guiding America through its history. From every fiery trial to each 'era of good feelings', God's providence steered this great nation down the course His hand had set. It was certainly evident in American history but we must not forget His hand in world affairs. God is in control of all of history, not just history pertaining to the United States. The same God that guided the course of

America guided the course of all other nations. He was even sovereign over empires such as Nazi Germany and Soviet Russia.

The early founders, minutemen and Continentals fought for liberty and justice. The Civil War was fought so that all men might enjoy these virtues. America went to war with some of the greatest empires in the world so that the inalienable rights of life, liberty and the pursuit of happiness might be preserved for generations to come.

You have just hit some of the high points of American history in this book. There are many more summits to climb. Connect with me at www.highpointhistoryseries.com to hit more high points!

Bibliography

Brezina, Corona. The Industrial Revolution in America: A Primary Source History of America's Transformation Into an Industrial Society. New York, New York: Rosen Publishing Group, 2005.

Burgan, Michael. The Missouri Compromise. Minneapolis, Minnesota: Compass Point Books,

2006.

Catel, Patrick. Battles of the Revolutionary War. Chicago, Illinois:

Heineman Publishing, 2011.

Childress, Diane. The War of 1812. Minneapolis, Minnesota: Lerner Publishing Company, 2004.

Chrisholm, Jane. The Usborne Book of World History Dates. London, England: Usborne Publishing, 1998.

Fradin, Dennis. The Signers.New York, New York: Walker Publishing Company, 2002.

Golay, Michael. Civil War. New York, New York: Facts on File, 2003.

Haberle, Susan. The Mexican War, 1846-1848. Mankato, Minnesota:

Capstone Press, 2003.

Herbert, Janis. The American Revolution For Kids. Chicago, Illinois: Chicago Review Press, 2002.

Maestro, Betsy. Struggle For A Continent. Singapore: Tien Wah Press, 2000.

Moriarty, J.T. The Rise of American Capitalism: The Growth of American Banks. New York, New York: Rosen Publishing Group, 2004.

Porterfield, Jason. Problems and Progress in American Politics: The Growth of the Democratic Party in the Late 1800s. New York, New York: Rosen Publishing Group, 2004.

Shea, Kitty. We The People: Industrial America. Minneapolis, Minnesota: Compass Point Books, 2005.

Sioux, Tracee. Immigration, Migration and the Industrial Revolution. New York, New York: Rosen Publishing Group, 2004.

Smith, Carter. Presidents of a Growing Country. The Millbrook Press, 1993.

Stites, Bill. The Republican Party of the Late 1800s: A Changing Role for American Government. New York, New York: Rosen Publishing Group, 2004.

The Kingfisher History Encyclopedia. New York, New York: Kingfisher Publications, 2004.

Urdang, Laurence. Timetables of American History. New York, New York: Touchstone Press, 1996.

Weir, William. 50 Battles That Changed the World. Franklin Lakes, New Jersey: The Career Press, 2004.

Wright, John. Timeline of the Civil War. London, United Kingdom: Amber Books Ltd., 2007.

Made in the USA
Lexington, KY
07 March 2016